# Reform and Reality

A Twentieth Century Fund Paper

# REFORM AND REALITY

## The Financing of State and Local Campaigns

by

Herbert E. Alexander

The Twentieth Century Fund Press / New York / 1991

The Twentieth Century Fund is a research foundation undertaking timely analyses of economic, political, and social issues. Not-for-profit and nonpartisan, the Fund was founded in 1919 and endowed by Edward A. Filene.

Library of Congress Cataloging-in-Publication Data

Alexander, Herbert E.
    Reform and reality: The financing of state and local campaigns/ by Herbert E. Alexander.
        p.        cm.
    "A Twentieth Century Fund paper."
    Includes bibliographical references and index.
    ISBN 0-87078-326-2 : $9.95
    1. Campaign funds—United States—States. 2. Local elections—United States—Finance.    I. Title.
    JK1991.A716    1991
    324.7'8'0973—dc20                                          91-37545
                                                                  CIP

# Foreword

The last two decades have been marked by dramatic changes in the rules of the game for American politics. At the federal, state, and local levels, an immense array of new laws and regulations affects the way campaigns are financed, how candidates are selected, and what information they are obligated to make public about themselves and their families. Though significant, these codified changes are probably less important than the changed expectations of the press and public concerning what is newsworthy and interesting about candidates and election campaigns. Most people would agree that all these changes, which are generally termed reforms, have been pointed in the right direction, improving the openness, honesty, and responsiveness of the political process.

Paradoxically, the public is even less happy with American politics today than it was at the beginning of this wave of changes a generation ago. We can only speculate on the reasons behind this unhappiness, but two come to mind. One is that however many formal changes have been made it would have been almost impossible for them to keep up with the informal changes in popular expectations and press coverage of political candidates and campaigns. The second reason is a bit more certain. With so many changes and different versions of reforms, it was always likely that some would fail or prove to be of limited usefulness along the road to some more acceptable set of rules of the game.

In this paper, Herbert Alexander, director of the Citizens' Research Foundation and professor of political science at the University of Southern California, reports on how some important American campaign finance reforms are working in states such as Michigan, Florida, New York, and California. This paper is the latest of many the Twentieth Century Fund has sponsored on this subject over the years, including *Voters' Time: Report of the Twentieth Century Fund Commission on Campaign Costs in the Electronic Age; Electing Congress: The Financial Dilemma*; and *What Price PACs?* The Fund also supported Larry Sabato's paper on campaign finance, *Paying for Elections*; Ross Baker's analysis of legislative PACs, *The New Fat Cats*; and Brooks Jackson's *Broken Promise: Why the Federal Election Commission Failed*. We intend to continue studying the way Americans elect their leaders and to persist in the search for a better way to pay for campaigns.

Herb Alexander, for three decades, has been more than an observer and scholar of these changes; he has been an active participant in shaping reforms in a number of jurisdictions across the country. The Fund is indebted to him for his insights into the process and for adding to the literature and our understanding of what is happening.

Richard C. Leone, PRESIDENT
The Twentieth Century Fund
October 1991

# Contents

# Acknowledgments

I want to acknowledge the assistance of the many state and local officials who so generously provided information and data. For reading and criticizing portions of the manuscript, special thanks are due to Dr. Frederick M. Herrmann, executive director of the New Jersey Election Law Enforcement Commission; Jeffrey M. Brindle, deputy director of ELEC; Frank P. Reiche, former chairman of ELEC; Professor Larry J. Sabato, University of Virginia; and Robert M. Stern, codirector and general counsel to the California Commission on Campaign Financing.

Louis M. Peck's assistance in the research and editing was invaluable. Without his guidance this publication would not have been possible.

Throughout, Gloria N. Cornette, assistant director of the Citizens' Research Foundation, was a constant source of help and strength, managing superbly the preparation of the manuscript at all stages.

A special note of thanks is due to Steven Greenfield, the editor at the Twentieth Century Fund, for his perceptive and meticulous assistance in preparing the manuscript for publication.

None of those who were so helpful is responsible for errors of omission or commission; for those, as for interpretations, the author bears sole responsibility.

# Introduction

At present, there are more than 520,000 elected officials holding office in the United States.[1] A mere one-tenth of 1 percent of this number—president, vice president, 100 members of the Senate, and 435 members of the House of Representatives—run for office under the financial strictures of the Federal Election Campaign Act. The remaining 99.9 percent, ranging from governors of megastates such as California and Florida to part-time trustees of tiny townships in the rural Midwest, are subject to a diverse patchwork of state and local laws in their quest for public office.

Although aspirants for state and local office spent in excess of $900 million in 1988—a figure that doubled in 1990 when there were many large-state governorships at stake—the attention of journalists and academics remains riveted on campaign finance at the federal level.[2] In contrast, scrutiny of the green in the political grass roots has been spotty, even though history shows the statehouse and the courthouse to be more scandal-prone when it comes to the interaction of money and influence.

The good news is that sensitivity toward impropriety, both actual and perceived, has made state legislatures and city councils more open to reform and experimentation than their counterparts in Congress. The situation mirrors the progressive era at the outset of the twentieth century, when numerous state legislatures, reacting to the excesses of the Gilded Age, enacted disclosure laws and prohibitions on corporate contributions more than a decade before Congress got around to taking such steps.

While Congress has not adopted significant campaign finance reform since the Watergate-induced changes of 1974, several states have moved in recent years to strengthen disclosure requirements or limit the size of campaign contributions. Some twenty-two states have enacted at least limited public financing for candidates or political parties during the decades of the 1970s and 1980s, as have such major municipalities as New York and Los Angeles.

Then there is the bad news.

Candidates for state and local office are being buffeted increasingly by the same financial pressures facing candidates at the federal level; it is just not as apparent because the relevant information, when publicly available, is fragmented and localized. The detail and availability of political finance disclosure by candidates vary widely from state to state, and there is no public entity to collect and analyze data from the fifty states in the manner in which the Federal Election Commission publishes spending totals and trends for presidential candidates and congressional aspirants.

This paper is an effort to fill some of those gaps, drawing upon available reporting and research on political finance at the state and local levels. Even more importantly, it is an attempt to highlight the issues that state legislatures and city councils must face if they are to reduce the opportunities for scandal while increasing the ability of those with modest means to seek public office.

There is no shortage of problems in this area:

❏ State and local campaign costs are skyrocketing. In California, the average cost of seeking a seat in the Assembly or state Senate now tops $500,000.[3] Even in rural Vermont, the median cost of a state Senate campaign jumped 50 percent from 1984 to 1988.[4]

❏ In many states, little has been done to limit campaign costs or donations. Only half a dozen states have systems in place to seek to contain overall expenditures. In twenty of the states, there are no limitations on how much an individual contributor may donate to a particular candidate, though such individual limits have been in place at the federal level since the post-Watergate reforms.

❏ As at the congressional level, state legislative candidates are becoming increasingly dependent on special interest money provided by a mushrooming number of political action committees, or PACs—probably some 12,000 of them—most linked to active lobby groups. The overwhelming majority of state-level PAC money is going to incumbents, and the resulting financial advantage has boosted reelection rates in many state legislatures above 96 percent—the same level of job security enjoyed by incumbent members of the U.S. House of Representatives seeking reelection in 1990.

❏ In states that have sought to limit the influence of special interest money through enactment of comprehensive public finance systems, an increasingly cynical citizenry has been loath to provide financing to candidates through checkoffs included as an option on taxpayers' returns. Meanwhile, spending limits in publicly funded statewide campaigns are being undercut by so-called soft money— money raised and spent outside contribution or expenditure limits—the same device that allowed George Bush and Michael Dukakis to spend twice the legislated spending ceiling in the 1988 presidential contest.

In some instances, reform has been stymied by judicial challenges testing the parameters of acceptable election law. In California, two campaign finance initiatives endorsed by the voters in June 1988 were the subject of a series of tangled court proceedings, and in Minnesota a recent effort to make state financing available to congressional candidates appears headed for court on constitutional grounds. Far from being considered obstructionist, the courts are to be commended for bringing understanding and clarity to the First Amendment issues of free speech and free association posed by the implied or explicit restrictions on political activity in some election laws.

In other states, the problem has been political rather than legal. The legislature in Maryland approved a public finance system but did not provide adequate funding—in part because those already in power do not relish the idea of providing financial assistance to those seeking to gain power; a similar situation occurred in Florida, but the legislature remedied the failure in 1991, after a five-year delay.

Those in power also do not like to pay to have themselves closely scrutinized. Consequently, the great majority of state election enforcement agencies are hamstrung by both a lack of authority and a lack of money. Even in New Jersey, which has the most generous public financing system for gubernatorial candidates of any state in the country, the state's Election Law Enforcement Commission has sustained serious cuts in budget in the past three fiscal years, paralleling reductions in other state agencies.

It is difficult, if not impossible, to formulate universally applicable solutions to resolve this list of concerns. No two states are alike in their political finance systems, any more than they are alike in their political culture and traditions. Any study must reflect the wide variety of approaches to reform. This paper seeks to provide some yardsticks with which to assess reforms already in place, and to measure proposed changes.

It may be helpful to consider such yardsticks at the outset in preparation for weighing the success—or lack thereof—of campaign reform in the states and localities whose experiences are detailed in the chapters to follow. The answers to the following questions can shed light on the efficacy of election reforms:

❏ Are more candidates seeking office?

❏ Are there more races that are competitive in terms of the ability of challengers to fund their campaigns adequately?

❏ Have the sources of campaign contributions changed appreciably?

❏ Have campaign contribution limits succeeded in decreasing the size of the average donation?

❏ Have campaign costs decreased?

❏ Have the fund-raising pressures on candidates decreased?

❏ Have opportunities for meaningful candidate/voter communications increased?

❏ Has the agency regulating elections been strengthened?

❏ Are disclosure reports sufficiently detailed and is the information summarized and widely available?

❏ Has the system increased public confidence and broadened public participation?

These questions should be asked not only about reforms already in place, but also about proposals for reform. Will the prospective reforms bring positive answers and further the goals of fairness, honesty, and democracy in electoral processes?

# Chapter 1

# As Goes California, So Goes the Nation

In 1962, in the Michigan city of Port Huron, Tom Hayden helped to found Students for a Democratic Society. In doing so, Hayden helped shape the politics of the moment, during which political power moved away from the legislative cloakrooms and party clubhouses and into the streets.

Twenty years later, Hayden again found himself on the cutting edge in defining the politics of the moment. This time, however, Hayden's tactics borrowed a page from a very traditional politician.

It was the late California Assembly speaker Jesse Unruh who coined the memorable phrase that "money is the mother's milk of politics." In 1982, when Hayden sought a seat in the California Assembly from the liberal enclave of Santa Monica, he pumped $2 million into the race by drawing on the financial resources of his then wife, actress Jane Fonda. He won. All told, Hayden and his general election opponent spent more than $3 million in pursuit of that office.[1]

But the real significance of Hayden's spending is apparent when it is placed in historical perspective. Just a quarter of a century earlier, in 1958, all legislative candidates combined spent $1.4 million in California. In 1982, Hayden alone outstripped this by 50 percent.

All told, spending on state legislative races in California in 1982 exceeded $43 million, more than double the $20.2 million expended in 1978. By 1986, that figure reached $57.1 million,[2] a 280 percent increase from just eight years earlier. That year, a race for an open Assembly seat in the Sacramento area came within shouting distance of Hayden's record, with the candidates spending a total of $2.4 million in the primary and general election.

However, in this instance, the financial angel was not Jane Fonda but Willie Brown, speaker of the California Assembly. And the money came not from acting fees or sales of aerobic exercise videos, but rather largely from many of the lobbying groups with interests before the state legislature. Brown's campaign committee, traditionally dependent on the largess of such groups, funneled more than $725,000 to its candidate in an unsuccessful effort to put the Sacramento seat in the Democratic column.[3]

By 1988, some $78.9 million was spent to elect the California legislature, although figures adjusted for transfers of funds would bring the total down to $61.1 million. Combining Senate and Assembly, the average amount spent by incumbents seeking reelection was $495,000, while average spending by general election winners was $599,000.[4] While spending in 1990 dipped downward to 1984–86 levels, there were large increases in amounts raised by legislative leaders and widening disparities between incumbents and challengers.

Undoubtedly, there will be an inclination by those from other regions of the country to dismiss these figures because they represent the experience of California, a sprawling, densely populated, and highly diverse state awash in political money from successful entrepreneurs and socially conscious entertainers. A former governor, Ronald Reagan, once noted that an independent California would have the world's seventh-largest gross national product.

But, in this instance, California is no mere aberration. When it comes to the trend lines of state and local campaign finance, there is increasing evidence to suggest that as goes California, so goes the nation.

In some parts of the country, the cost of mounting a state legislative campaign is beginning to resemble that of a highly competitive congressional bid, notwithstanding the fact that many state legislatures officially remain only part-time operations. In California in 1988, the most expensive general election campaign was that of state Senator Cecil Green, who spent $1.4 million—against $1 million for his opposition—successfully defending a seat he won the year before in a multimillion-dollar special election. In the 1986 race for the Florida Senate, one candidate spent more than $447,461 in the primary and general election. A year later, an aspirant for the state Senate in New Jersey expended $378,000. In 1988, a candidate for the Washington state Senate spent more than $237,000.[5] And in 1990, a Pennsylvania state senator spent $750,000 in an unsuccessful effort to save his seat.

As Gary Moncrief of Boise State University wryly observed in a 1990 study of the costs of legislative elections, "In some states, the increase in the value of a legislative seat seems to be on the same curve as the Los Angeles real estate market."[6] Of course, sometimes the contest is not only for a single seat but for party control of a house of the legislature, where the stakes may be high indeed. And while the Los Angeles real estate market has receded a bit, the value of increasing party presence in the state legislature remains relatively high.

## State Campaign Costs: Higher and Higher, Coast-to-Coast

In a 1984 article on the financing of state elections, Ruth Jones of Arizona State University declared: "State election campaign costs, especially for legislative races, are rapidly escalating beyond any increases that may be related to inflation."[7] The cost spiral has not slowed. In 1988, spending on contests for statewide office and state legislative seats reached $540 million, as compared with about $120 million in 1976,[8] a 450 percent increase in just twelve years. Figure 1 demonstrates that the costs of running for state office have outstripped the rates of spending for presidential, congressional or local elections.

This phenomenon has affected states with widely different population sizes, demographics, and political leanings. A survey by the National

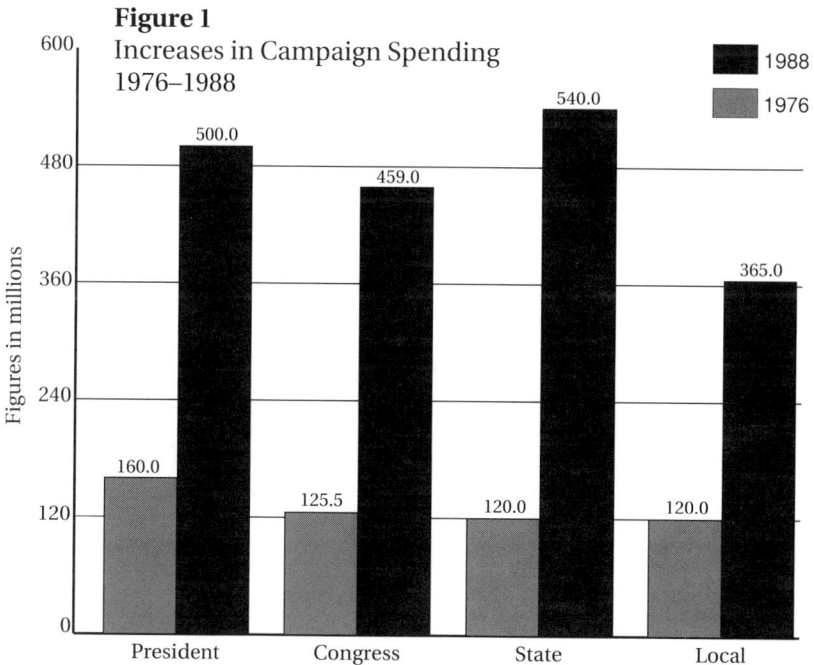

**Figure 1**

Increases in Campaign Spending 1976–1988

Figures in millions

| President | Congress | State | Local |
|-----------|----------|-------|-------|
| 160.0 / 500.0 | 125.5 / 459.0 | 120.0 / 540.0 | 120.0 / 365.0 |

■ 1988
▨ 1976

Sources: Citizens' Research Foundation and Federal Election Commission.

Conference of State Legislatures (NCSL) measured the rise in the median cost of seeking state legislative office during the mid-1980s, a period of limited inflation. In the case of the Alaska Senate, primary and general election costs rose 219 percent and 140 percent, respectively, between 1982 and 1988. In Oregon, the comparable increases were 239 percent and 157 percent. For the Florida Senate, combined primary and general election costs jumped 123 percent between 1982 and 1986. General election costs for the Connecticut Senate were up 80 percent during that same period.[9]

Even the smallest of states is not immune. While the chief counsel of the Vermont General Assembly claimed not long ago that "you can run on as much as it takes to put gas in your Volkswagen to drive around knocking on people's doors,"[10] the NCSL survey shows that the median cost of running for the Vermont Senate rose 52 percent between 1982 and 1988.

Moncrief's exhaustive study of legislative costs in Idaho, Montana, Oregon, and Washington offers further evidence of this trend. With inflation taken into account, the average expenditure per candidate still increased almost 300 percent in races for the Oregon Senate, 150 percent in contests for the Oregon House, and more than 90 percent in Washington Senate campaigns between 1980 and 1988. Even in states such as Idaho and Montana, where the concept of the "citizen-legislature" persists, Moncrief found inflation-adjusted increases of 11 to 30 percent during the early to mid-1980s.[11]

When it comes to statewide contests, particularly for governor, the pattern of increase is somewhat less consistent. One explanation is that, while there always are a certain number of legislative seats hotly contested by the two major parties, entrenched governors may face little more than token opposition. However, when a gubernatorial contest involves an open seat or vulnerable incumbent, costs have been rising on a curve similar to or exceeding state legislative contests.

In fact, it appears that the cost of running for governor is, on average, outstripping that of the other major statewide officeholder, U.S. senator, elected under federal rather than state election laws. In 1986, the average cost of a gubernatorial election, including primary and general elections, reached $7 million.[12] Based on data filed with the Federal Election Commission, the average total for U.S. Senate seats that year was slightly more than $6.2 million per race.

In Florida, candidates seeking the open gubernatorial seat in 1986 spent more than $24 million, including primary and general elections. Figures for other open seats that year included $16 million in Pennsylvania and

$14.6 million in Tennessee. A year later, in the Kentucky governor's race, more than $12 million was spent in the Democratic primary alone. Because Kentucky governors by law are not allowed to succeed themselves, the state provides a stark example of the escalating costs when an open seat is at stake. Between 1975 and 1987, spending in the Kentucky Democratic gubernatorial primary almost quadrupled even after factoring in inflation.[13]

In Texas in 1986, when Democratic incumbent Mark White—rendered vulnerable by the weak southwestern economy—was ousted by Republican ex-governor William Clements, the candidates spent a total of $35 million. That record level did not stand for long. In 1990, with Clements retiring, candidates spent a total of $50.5 million for primary and general elections combined. An even higher amount for 1990—$53.2 milion—was recorded in California, for all primary and general election candidates for governor. Following California and Texas, the next-highest totals were only about half as much, $25.1 million in Florida and $23.9 million in Illinois. For all thirty-five states with gubernatorial campaigns in 1990, total campaign costs were $345.5 million.[14] (The all-time record may have been set in 1966, when a reported $10 million was spent by Nelson Rockefeller's reelection campaign for governor of New York; in terms of the value of the dollar then and now, this remains unparalleled for a single candidate.)

Proportionately, smaller states are being affected in much the same manner. In 1988, the candidates for governor of Montana spent a total of $2.7 million. That may not sound like much given that greater sums are being spent on attempts to win a single Assembly seat in California. But that $2.7 million greatly increases in significance, considering that it is more than was spent by all statewide and state legislative candidates in Montana just four years earlier.[15]

## The Political Cost of Large Campaign Expenditures

There is no single, straightforward explanation for the geometric progression of these increases. And there is by no means unanimity on whether these costs can—or should—be curtailed. Some even argue that not enough is being spent, seeing that less than 50 percent of the electorate bothers to vote and that those who do often have only the most cursory knowledge of the issues at stake.

What is not in dispute is that escalating costs have forced serious candidates into a continuous search for new supplies of campaign cash. Obviously, this has placed candidates with fortunes at their disposal at a distinct advantage.

Tom Hayden is but one example. The same year that Hayden captured his Assembly seat, Republican Lewis Lehrman took more than $8 million of the fortune derived from the Rite Aid drugstore empire and put it into an effort to become governor of New York. Lehrman lost narrowly in his first bid for elective office. In 1990, Clayton Williams spent some $9 million of his personal fortune in a $20 million unsuccessful bid for the Texas governorship. Two of the last three governors of Kentucky, John Y. Brown and Wallace Wilkinson, are self-made millionaires who parlayed their fortunes into victory during their first tries for office. To win the Democratic primary, which has proven tantamount to winning recent Kentucky gubernatorial contests, Brown and Wilkinson lent their campaigns $1.25 million and $2.3 million, respectively.[16] John Y. Brown sought to turn his ability to finance himself to his political advantage, campaigning as the candidate who "could not be bought."

However, most candidates seeking statewide and state legislative office cannot fund their own campaigns, and their pursuit of wealthy individuals and special interest lobbies is creating a perception that the financing system is corrupt. Unfortunately, this is yet another example where California is quite representative of the nation as a whole. A poll by the *Los Angeles Times* found that voters, by a margin of 2-to-1, agreed with the statement that "most state legislators are for sale to their largest campaign contributors."[17]

A recently released report by the New Jersey legislature's Ad Hoc Commission on Legislative Ethics and Campaign Finance, in identifying problems in the current system of campaign finance, spoke of "a public perception that public officials and candidates are influenced in their actions and opinions, perhaps inordinately, by the persons, companies or organizations who make large or numerous contributions of money to their election or re-election campaigns." The commission report also cited "a public perception that excessive fundraising for election or re-election distracts elected officials from governing and gives the impression that the official's vote is for sale to the contributors making the largest donations."[18]

Such perceptions are hardly unique to the state level. Polls showing members of Congress to be held in low regard by the voters have generated debate about the current system of federal campaign finance for many years. But the problem is even more acute at the state and local levels, where laws governing the size and source of contributions tend to be less stringent.

It is hard to generalize because restrictions vary widely from state to state. But, at last count, twenty states put no limits on the amount that can be contributed to a candidate by any one individual, while congressional candidates may accept no more than $1,000 from any one individual per election.[19] It is noteworthy, however, that a number of states in recent years have moved to impose similar limits.

A quarter of the states still allow unlimited direct contributions from corporations, a practice banned altogether at the federal level since the passage of the Tillman Act during the administration of Theodore Roosevelt. Almost half of the states put no limit on direct contributions from labor unions; the federal government has not permitted direct labor union contributions to candidates for more than forty years.

Of course, corporate and labor interests give generously to federal candidates by use of political action committees (PACs). But these committees can give no more than $10,000 per election cycle to candidates for Congress. In half of the states, there are still no limits on the amount that a state PAC—sometimes known as a separate segregated fund, or SSF—can give to a candidate.

As will be discussed later, this setup benefits incumbents at the state and local levels much as it aids sitting members of Congress. Consequently, while a number of state legislatures have moved in recent years to limit special interest contributions and make alternative resources—such as public funding—available to candidates, many state legislators have had little incentive to disturb the current system.

That point was brought home by John D. Feerick, chairman of the New York Commission on Government Integrity. Appointed in 1987 amid burgeoning scandals in the New York City government, the commission undertook an extensive and praiseworthy program of research and publication. The commission ceased operations in September 1990 with praise for the city's adoption of sweeping campaign finance and ethics reform. But Feerick leveled a sharp blast at the state legislature.

"The laws of New York state fall woefully short in guarding against political abuses in an alarming number of areas," he declared, adding, "The state's failure to address in particular the subject of campaign finance is a disgrace and embarrassment."

Charging that the state's contribution limits—$50,000 for individuals—"are so high that to call them limits is a mockery," Feerick concluded: "The result is cynicism about government, distrust, and ultimately a lack of integrity in government."[20]

### Virginia as Case Study: Fat Cat Redux

The 1989 gubernatorial election in the Commonwealth of Virginia marked a milestone in American history: Democrat L. Douglas Wilder became the first black man in modern American history to reach the governor's mansion. What made the achievement all the more remarkable was that it occurred in a state that was the capital of the old Confederacy.

But the contest also was noteworthy for some less lofty reasons. First, the four candidates who actively sought the governorship— Wilder and the three Republicans who engaged in a bitter primary for the right to oppose him—spent a total of $25.7 million, more than two and half times what was spent during the 1985 gubernatorial contest. The 1989 Virginia race was in the same price range as 1986 gubernatorial battles in California and Florida, states with populations far more numerous than the Old Dominion.[21]

The other distinguishing characteristic of the Virginia race, financially speaking, was the candidates' dependence on large contributors. During the Republican primary, in which former state attorney general J. Marshall Coleman bested former senator Paul Trible and Representative Stanford Parris, each candidate raised more than half his money in gifts of $10,000 or more.[22] Meanwhile, more than 10 percent of the $6.9 million taken in by Wilder was directly contributed or raised by John Kluge, a media magnate who is one of America's wealthiest men.

Virginia is illustrative of what can happen when, in an era of escalating campaign costs, nothing is done to curtail candidates' demands for less desirable forms of political money. The state has absolutely no contribution limits: individuals, corporations, labor unions, and banks are free to contribute as they see fit. There is an income tax add-on option, which aids political parties modestly, but there is no system for providing public funds directly to candidates in order to reduce reliance on large contributors.

The result was that both Coleman and Wilder turned to several large donors whose financial well-being was at least partially dependent on the actions of government.

Coleman, who lost to Wilder in the closest gubernatorial race in Virginia history, raised more than $11 million. Almost 15 percent of that came from three men who have made fortunes in the real estate boom that has enveloped the northern Virginia suburbs of Washington, D.C., in recent years. One of these men, Dwight Schar of McLean, Virginia, was Coleman's largest single contributor; he and his family donated more than $700,000 to the Coleman effort[23] and lent another $250,000 that was repaid after the primary. His 1989 net worth was estimated at $100 million by *Virginia Business* magazine.

Schar is a neighbor of Coleman's. According to Securities and Exchange Commission records, Coleman's law firm received $4.7 million in legal fees from Schar over a three-year period. That was not Coleman's only financial connection to Schar and his firm, NVRyan. The *Washington Post* reported during the campaign that Coleman earned about $100,000 in 1988 and 1989 by buying and reselling homes built by Schar, and that Schar in 1984 had offered Coleman a share of the profit from one project if Coleman could persuade local officials to change the zoning regulations in the developer's favor.[24] Coleman was unsuccessful in doing so.

While the *Post* reported that about 40 percent of Coleman's funding was coming from development interests,[25] Wilder was not without some significant support from this sector. One of Wilder's six-figure contributors was an Iranian immigrant named Bahman Batmanghelidj, a developer with several projects in the northern Virginia region.

Batmanghelidj came under scrutiny in 1989, when it was disclosed that he received a $78 million loan guarantee from the federal Department of Housing and Urban Development (HUD) after paying $1 million to hire several consultants with Republican connections—including the wife of then White House aide Joseph Canzeri. A subsequent report by the HUD inspector general cleared Batmanghelidj of wrongdoing, although it questioned whether HUD officials were justified in providing the loan guarantee.

Batmanghelidj repeatedly insisted that he wanted nothing from Wilder for his contribution, and invoked the name and ideals of one of Virginia's most distinguished sons, Thomas Jefferson, in explaining the donation. "If Doug Wilder is elected, Mr. Jefferson still lives," he asserted.[26] Likewise Schar, asked what he wanted in return for his contribution to Coleman, replied, "Good government."[27] Nevertheless, their contributions came at a time when the real estate industry was asking the state to block attempts by local governments in northern Virginia to curtail development. Interestingly, both Wilder and Coleman took positions during the campaign that sided with the real estate industry.

Wilder's biggest contributor was John Kluge, a Charlottesville billionaire who—depending on calculations—is the first or second wealthiest person in America. Kluge, whose fortune was built in radio and television, personally donated $200,000 to Wilder; he and his then wife, Patricia, held fund-raisers that produced another $600,000 for Wilder's campaign.[28] At the time, Kluge had invested in a group seeking state approval to build a horse racing track.

While the Democrats sought to make an issue of Coleman's ties to Schar, the Republicans sought to do the same with Wilder and the Kluges. They complained of Wilder's predecessor, Democrat Gerald Baliles, spending $250,000 on a Charlottesville film festival in October 1988 that the GOP characterized as a "private party" for Patricia Kluge. They also charged that Patricia Kluge was trying to buy her way on to the University of Virginia's Board of Visitors, one of the state's most coveted political appointments.[29] (Ms. Kluge was appointed to the board shortly after Wilder's inauguration.)

University of Virginia professor Larry Sabato noted that the size of the contributions in the gubernatorial race approached the million-dollar donations made to presidential candidates in the late 1960s and early 1970s by such individuals as W. Clement Stone. Stone's large gifts to Richard Nixon were a factor in congressional passage of the 1974 law to curtail the influence of large donors by placing strict limits on individual contributions in presidential and congressional elections.

"We've reached the W. Clement Stone level," Sabato said of Virginia, "and there's no end in sight."[30] Several bills to limit contributions to Virginia statewide and state legislative candidates were introduced following the Wilder–Coleman race. But no action was taken by the Virginia legislature until 1991, when the state enacted a bill requiring disclosure of political party contributions and expenditures.

## Behind the Rising Costs

### The Allure of State Office

The ample supply of large contributors in growing states such as California and Virginia helps to explain the rapid rise in campaign costs. But it is far from being the only explanation, and is an outgrowth of the problem as much as a root cause. There are a multiplicity of determinants behind the increases, only some of which lend themselves to legislation.

Public office both at the statewide and state legislative levels seems to have grown in desirability over the past decade. The "New Federalism" of the Reagan administration in the early 1980s placed increased responsibility for governing at the statehouse level. Several leading issues of the 1980s concerned areas like education, where the state rather than the federal government has traditionally had the lion's share of the jurisdiction. Furthermore, many regions of the country enjoyed healthy economies throughout much of the past decade, providing state governments with ample revenue and scope for experimentation and innovation.

It is noteworthy that in the past several years, two U.S. senators (Republicans Paul Trible of Virginia and Pete Wilson of California) decided that the governorship is a preferable alternative to "the world's most exclusive club." It also is notable that two of the last three presidents (Jimmy Carter and Ronald Reagan) ascended to the White House from the governor's mansion rather than from the Senate, and that the Democratic party nominee in 1988, Michael Dukakis, was a sitting governor.

Meanwhile, state legislators who once would have jumped at the opportunity to move up to the U.S. House of Representatives now often find such a move less enticing. The formidable incumbent reelection rate in both state legislatures and the U.S. House acts as a strong deterrent. In other words, why give up a safe state legislative seat for the decidedly dicey prospect of taking on a congressional incumbent?

Even if the congressional seat opens up through retirement, there are drawbacks, particularly for Republicans. The House has been under unbroken Democratic control for almost forty years, and the chances that will change anytime soon—the forthcoming 1992 reapportionment notwithstanding—are debatable. Senior Republican state legislators in bodies with a clear GOP tilt, perhaps holding the chair of a major committee, are reluctant to give that up to go to Washington and become a member of a seemingly permanent minority.

### The Professionalization of State Legislative Campaigns

The increased responsibility placed upon state legislatures and the enhanced political desirability of state legislative seats contributed to what has been termed a "congressionalization" of some legislatures. Just as members of Congress consider that to be their full-time pursuit—indeed, current ethics laws force them to consider the job that way—many state senators and assemblymen are coming to regard themselves as professional politicians rather than Jeffersonian "citizen-legislators."

When politics becomes one's chief livelihood, rather than an activity to be engaged in for a sixty-day legislative session every other year, there is more at stake in protecting that livelihood by fending off opponents in primaries and general elections. Thus, the door has opened wide for the professionalization of campaigning. State legislators who a generation ago walked around the district passing out combs and pencils bearing their names are now hiring full-time campaign managers, advertising specialists, and direct mail experts.

Gary Moncrief's recent study of four northwestern state legislatures found a correlation between professionalization and the rate of campaign spending increase. Besides measuring average expenditures per candidate, which he found to have increased in all four legislatures, Moncrief also broke down spending totals per legislative seat.

"The value of a legislative seat has increased in both chambers in Washington and Oregon, but has remained almost constant in Idaho and Montana," he wrote. From 1980 to 1988, the constant-dollar value of a seat in the Oregon Senate more than tripled, while it almost doubled in the Oregon House and Washington Senate. "Both Oregon and Washington are at the mid-range in terms of professionalism, and there are probably a number of legislators in both states who now claim 'legislator' as their primary occupation," he added. "Montana and Idaho, on the other hand, are still characterized as 'citizen-legislatures.' . . ."[31]

The professionalization of state legislative campaigns has gotten a push from the national committees of both major parties, which once all but ignored such races. With the continuing shift of population from the Northeast and Midwest to the South and West, the political stakes in congressional reapportionment have grown—and it is state legislatures that redraw the maps for U.S. House districts after every decennial census. The Democratic National Committee (DNC) was expected to spend at least $5 million between 1985 and 1990 on state legislative campaigns, and the better-financed Republican National Committee spent even more than that.[32]

"As these races have become increasingly expensive, we have had to drive in even more money, and find people who know how to spend the money," said Tim Dickson of Project 500, the DNC's reapportionment program. "We have tried to take [state] legislative campaigns into targeting, polling and direct mail and out of rain hats, combs, mirrors and emery boards."[33]

The political tactics used by legislative campaigns differ significantly from statewide efforts, which are now relying almost exclusively on television. In the 1990 Texas gubernatorial race, GOP candidate Clayton Williams so saturated the airwaves that by some estimates his spot announcements had been seen some eighty times by the average Texan.[34] By comparison, state legislative districts generally do not fall neatly within media markets, and so expensive television advertising would be wasted on noneligible voters.

However, the cost of state legislative campaigns is being driven increasingly by direct mail, as consultants are able to break a district down into hundreds of subdemographic groups. "You give me a group, and I'll guarantee you that three times out of four, I can find the people in that group who are going to support my candidate or my issue," Richie Ross, one of California's top political consultants, boasted not long ago.[35]

While the emphasis on direct mail was first practiced in California's large, ethnically diverse, state legislative districts, the practice has spread east. In 1987, with control of the New Jersey Senate at stake, then Senate president John Russo created a PAC that raised $1.8 million by Election Day. The money went to hire consultants to assist in retaining or electing Democrats in twelve "swing" seats. "Direct mail served as the primary vehicle of communication between candidate and voter," wrote two consultants who participated in the effort. "The 12 campaigns averaged nine different direct mail pieces; all totaled, they produced over four million pieces of mail, more than half of which dropped less than three weeks before Election Day. So much mail was dropped that the consultants set up informal operations in a local bar across the street from the Newark post office."[36]

This strategy, under which the legislative leadership targets certain seats crucial to maintaining or achieving majority control, is being employed increasingly throughout the country. While one legislative candidate in a medium-sized or small state may find veteran consultants beyond his or her means, the targeted and coordinated approach enables pooled money to be used to hire consultants to work for several campaigns. In New Jersey, Russo's PAC brought in more than half a dozen outside consultants to handle media, polling, and demographic targeting and mailing as well as to set up sophisticated phone bank operations.[37]

There is mixed evidence on the degree to which this practice has raised the cost of highly competitive races as compared with other legislative contests. However, in some instances it has translated into very high costs even in the least professionalized of legislatures. In Idaho in 1988, more than $240,000 was spent by both sides as the Democrats succeeded in ousting the Republican president pro tempore of the state Senate.[38] That is about twenty times the average for all other Idaho Senate seats.

## A New Kind of Arms Race

Even when there is not a competitive election, candidates for statewide and state legislative office increasingly feel obligated to raise and spend large amounts of money to scare off opponents or guard against eleventh-hour surprises. This has given rise to what critics call an "arms race" mentality in campaign finance. While straining the military metaphor a bit, the California Commission on Campaign Financing was on target when it wrote in 1985:

> Candidates fear that opponents will outspend them, that first strikes will overwhelm them, that last-minute attacks will unseat them, and that innovations will make their contemporary weapons and defenses obsolete. Candidates turn to deterrence, the massive buildup of money and arms, for security.[39]

Mario Cuomo, current New York governor and perhaps a future presidential candidate, is an example of that kind of thinking. Cuomo has not had a serious election opponent since 1982, when Lewis Lehrman came within four points of denying him the statehouse. In 1986, Cuomo was reelected by a record margin. In 1990, his Republican opponent, economist Pierre Rinfret, almost pulled out of the race due to lack of financial support stemming from an ongoing feud with state GOP leaders. Cuomo still felt compelled to spend at least $2 million on television advertising, and did not win by as large a margin as in 1986.[40]

The situation was similar in Maryland. Popular Democratic incumbent William Donald Schaefer, seeking reelection in 1990, faced an unknown Republican opponent, William Shepard. The Republican candidate caused chuckles among the Democrats and outrage within his own party by choosing his wife as the lieutenant gubernatorial nominee, and had raised all of $100,000 by mid-October. But Schaefer, a longtime Baltimore mayor prior to the governorship, facing what was all but certain to be his final bid for elective office, felt compelled to raise more than $2.3 million even in the face of such opposition.[41]

While information on trends in local campaign finance is more limited than state-level data, there are numerous indications that a similar escalation is occurring in races for city and county officials. Although the overall increase in spending on local races was not as dramatic as that for statewide and state legislative office, it still jumped threefold from $120 million to $365 million between 1976 and 1988.[42] The professionalization of campaigns for mayor, city council, and county supervisor, while occurring nationwide, is particularly prevalent in the growing cities of the South and West.

"In a California city that had 30,000 people 30 years ago and today has a quarter of million, you don't have a reputation," observed former Fresno mayor Daniel Whitehurst. "What you have, maybe, is an image. And if you don't have one, you go out and buy one."[43]

In a 1989 report, the California Commission on Campaign Financing found that an average of 10 percent of each local campaign dollar is spent on consultants. It went on to complain that, in numerous municipalities, "candidates exhibit the worst excesses of a system drunk with cash. They isolate themselves from the voters, rely on phalanxes of paid political advisors, raise contributions around the clock, accumulate huge warchests in non-election years, scare off challengers, solicit contributions from persons with financial interests pending before them, spend large sums of money on entertainment, fundraising and travel, and communicate with the public through orchestrated media campaigns."[44]

## Paying the Price

Who is footing the bill for this seemingly endless cost spiral? As noted in the account of the 1989 Virginia gubernatorial race, wealthy individual contributors play an important role in the states allowing unlimited donations to a candidate. But a second major source of funding has emerged in recent years: political action committees representing corporations, unions, trade associations, and membership groups with interests before state legislatures.

This is yet another aspect of the "congressionalization" of state legislative campaigns. Just as candidates for the U.S. Senate and House are more dependent on PAC contributions than they were in the mid-1970s, so has PAC involvement in statehouse races sharply increased. (See Figure 2.)

The California Commission on Campaign Financing reports that from 1980 through 1984, legislative candidates received an average of 56 percent of their contributions either from PACs or directly from labor unions and businesses.[45] This trend held steady during the 1986 legislative elections. The commission notes that businesses, unions, and PACs actually increased their donations by one-third between the 1984 and 1986 election cycles, but that their overall share remained about the same (53 percent)[46] because of the large increase in cash from national party committees.

Again, California is hardly an exception. The Maryland chapter of Common Cause, in a report published in the fall of 1990, found that PAC contributions to state legislative candidates during 1986–90 almost doubled over the 1982–86 period.[47] The number of PACs giving to Maryland statewide elected officials as well as legislative candidates jumped by 50 percent over the previous four-year period.

According to a September 1990 report by Common Cause, the organization found a similar pattern in other states in various regions of the country. In Colorado, PACs accounted for 62 percent of the donations to House candidates in 1986. In Oregon that year, PACs contributed almost three-quarters of the money in legislative races in the primary and general elections. And in the 1988 elections for the Michigan legislature, 69 percent of the donations came from PACs, up from 58 percent just two years before.

"There is no definitive accounting of the number of political action committees active in state level elections, nor do we know the full amount of their collective contributions," Ruth Jones writes. "However, all 50 states report ever increasing PAC involvement in the financing of campaigns, both in terms of the PACs and the amounts being contributed."[48]

**Figure 2**

Legislative Fund-Raising: The Role of Interest Groups

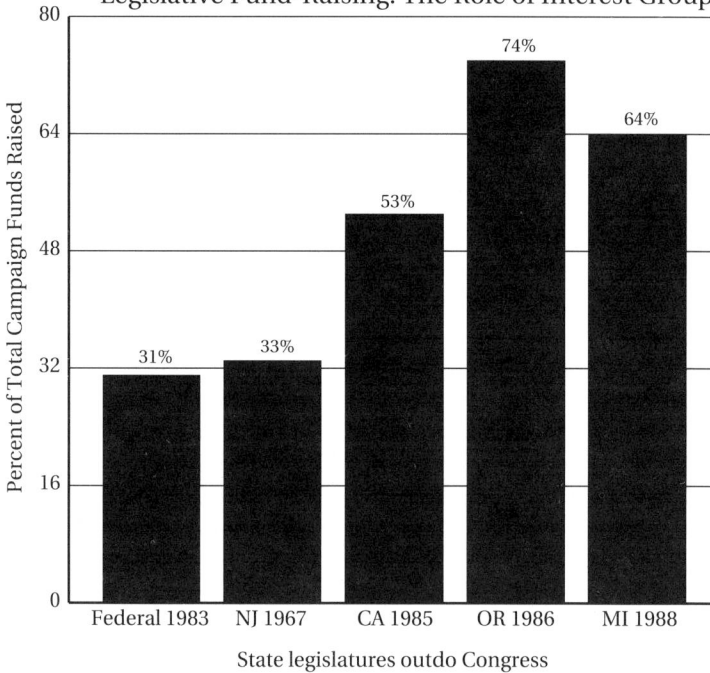

State legislatures outdo Congress

Sources: Compiled from Federal Election Commission; New Jersey
Election Law Enforcement Commission; California Commission on
Campaign Financing; Common Cause.

Jones notes that New Jersey reported a 118 percent increase in the number of state-level PACs between 1983 and 1987, while there was an 87 percent jump in the amount that PACs contributed to candidates.

As at the federal level, defenders of the state PAC system claim that the influence of such donations is neutralized because there are so many PACs with competing interests giving to many of the same candidates. Such arguments, however, are dismissed even by those who have accepted large amounts from such groups. "It goes beyond the ability of anyone being able to say that these kinds of contributions don't have an influence," says California Assembly speaker Willie Brown.[49]

And candidates are not simply sitting back and watching as interest group donations roll in; they are aggressively seeking them out. As will be seen in Chapter 2, lobbyists complain of being strong-armed and threatened with legislation adverse to their interest (so-called juice bills) unless they are forthcoming with donations. This practice extends to those seeking statewide office. During the 1990 election, the Birmingham *Post-Herald* reported that Alabama governor Guy Hunt threatened to withhold state contracts from businesses that did not support his campaign exclusively. Hunt reportedly told about 150 business executives invited to the governor's mansion that financial disclosure statements would be scrutinized to enforce his edict.[50]

Two years earlier, the New York Commission on Government Integrity held hearings on the operations of state comptroller Edward V. Regan, during which it was disclosed that more than 90 percent of the contributions to Regan over a five-year period came from companies doing business with his office. In one memo released by the commission, a top aide to Regan complained about the low level of giving by one firm that had received almost a quarter of a million dollars in fees. "We do an enormous amount of business with the firm, yet they more or less refused to return the favor."[51] The commission also criticized Governor Mario Cuomo and Attorney General Robert Abrams for soliciting contributions from state contractors.

Louisiana's flamboyant ex-governor, Edwin Edwards, made little effort to hide such practices. After regaining the governorship in 1983, Edwards invited Louisiana's political, social, and business elite to take a weeklong trip back to his Cajun roots: France. About 450 Louisianans, many of them lobbyists, paid $10,000 a head for "Le Retour aux Notre Sources avec Notre Gouverneur Edwards," which included a night at the Lido and a mass at Notre Dame.

It was far more than a sentimental journey; the profits from the trip were used to pay off a $4 million campaign debt that Edwards had accumulated. "There are two kinds of people on this trip—those who can afford it and those who have to afford it," remarked an Edwards aide.[52] Edwards, who was tried twice on corruption charges during his 1983–87 term, was defeated for reelection by Representative Charles (Buddy) Roemer, who successfully pushed for legislation to reform the state's wide-open system of campaign finance.

While the intersection of donations and influence has shaken public confidence in the operation of state government, it also has produced actual as well as perceived corruption. In early 1990, state senator Joseph Montoya became the first California legislator convicted of a felony in a third of a century. As part of a continuing FBI "sting" operation in Sacramento, Montoya was found guilty of using his position to extort funds from lobbyists representing foreign medical schools.

Several months later, a second legislator, former state senator Paul Carpenter, was convicted. The Carpenter case is noteworthy because, unlike Montoya, Carpenter was not accused of selling his vote or putting the money in his pocket. Rather, Carpenter was convicted of selling "access"—his time, energy, and attention—in return for a $20,000 campaign contribution from an FBI undercover agent.[53]

Meanwhile, almost 3,000 miles away, another FBI sting operation in the South Carolina state capital had netted fourteen legislators as of early 1991, with seven pleading guilty or convicted of bribery charges. And in Arizona, six legislators were indicted after being videotaped accepting cash payoffs, while a seventh pleaded guilty.

If there is no empirical way to measure corruption at the state and local levels, it is nonetheless undoubtedly greater than at the federal level because more of the direct contracting of services is handled at the grass roots. In addition, the presence of a few dominant interests in many states and municipalities increases the chance that an official will become heavily dependent on such interests. The nation's two largest cities are a case in point.

A study by New York state senator Franz Leichter found that during the 1985 New York City elections, real estate interests gave about $4 million to members of the city's powerful Board of Estimate. That body, which was abolished in 1990 after the Supreme Court found it violated the principle of "one-person, one-vote," had the power to grant zoning variances and city leases. Eight of the ten top contributors to the Board of Estimate members in 1985 were major real estate developers.

"These contributors are hard-headed businessmen," Leichter told the *Wall Street Journal.* "They don't give because they like the positions of board members on Israel, gay rights or abortion." At the same time, the head of a trade association representing New York developers complained that "the pressure on the real-estate community to give money to the campaigns is rather intense."[54]

Meanwhile, a 1985 *Los Angeles Times* study found that 25 percent of the donors to city mayoral campaigns were in real estate, and that more than 40 percent "either do business with the city or need the city's approval for work that they or their clients want to undertake."[55]

**The Statehouse Transfer**

Increasingly, contributions from interest groups are not only going directly to rank-and-file legislators, but also are flowing into campaign committees set up by legislative leaders. The leaders then shift the money to incumbent legislators and challengers in need of assistance, just as California Assembly speaker Brown's committee provided $725,000 in the 1986 race for the open Sacramento area Assembly seat.

These "transfers," which remain unrestricted in most states, are controversial. Supporters say that they strengthen the role of political parties and help impose discipline on state legislative bodies that, like Congress, are becoming "every person for himself or herself" operations in which it is difficult to achieve consensus. Critics counter that the practice gives inordinate power to legislative leaders. Just as the prevalence of PAC contributions makes a legislator beholden to corporate and labor interests, transfers indebt that legislator to a leader rather than his or her own constituents, the critics say. Leadership fund-raising, if not done on behalf of party committees, creates a "personality cult" devoted to personal ambition or to factional strength rather than to revitalizing the parties.

The California Commission on Campaign Financing wrote in 1985: "Legislative leaders feel themselves under increasing pressure to raise and transfer larger and larger sums of money. They often do so by soliciting contributions from individuals and organizations who are affected by legislation and are willing to contribute money to influence its outcome."[56] By 1986, California legislative candidates were depending on transfers for almost 40 percent of their money, and more than 90 percent of this was coming from committees set up by legislative leaders and other officeholders.[57] The practice was prohibited by California's Proposition 73 in 1988. But a federal judge, ruling on a suit by Democratic party leaders and unions, in late 1990 invalidated many of Proposition 73's restrictions (see Chapter 3).

Another large state where the use of transfers has received attention is Ohio, in which House Speaker Vernal Riffe holds an annual "birthday party." This device has taken in more than $1 million to distribute to favored candidates.[58] A recent analysis by the *Akron Beacon Journal* disclosed that committees controlled by Riffe and state Senate president Stanley Aronoff had received at least a half million dollars in "pipeline" contributions from corporations trying to influence the legislative process. Such donations, while collected from company employees and bundled together in one corporate donation, show up in disclosure reports as donations from individual employees. They are, therefore, difficult to trace.

The *Beacon Journal* report said that more than $275,000 of these contributions came from Ohio utility companies during a two-year period "when utilities were enjoying enviable success in pushing bills through the General Assembly."[59]

Meanwhile, much of the campaign money collected by Ohio legislators is being used for expenses that have little to do with campaigning. Another *Akron Beacon Journal* report noted that legislators are furiously collecting donations, only to spend them on such items as Christmas party liquor, membership in the National Rifle Association, lawn-care services, and tickets to Ohio State football games—not to communicate with voters or constituents.[60]

### The Permanent State Legislature

Besides spawning corruption or the appearance of corruption and shaking public confidence, the greatest political cost of the current system of campaign finance is that of denying opportunity to those who want to serve the public. As with the House of Representatives, it is growing more and more difficult to win election to state legislatures. Consequently, many able newcomers may not even be trying.

The inherent advantages of incumbency are exacerbated by the power of special interest contributions from PACs or lobbyists, as well as direct contributions from corporations and unions because the funds are directed more and more to incumbents. At the congressional level, about three-quarters of this money goes to incumbents. Available evidence indicates that the percentage is even higher in some states.

The recent analysis by Common Cause/Maryland shows that, between November 1986 and August 1990, incumbents in statewide office and the state legislature received 89 percent of the money donated by PACs over a four-year period.[61] In Massachusetts in 1988, some 81 percent of the money contributed to all incumbents came from PACs, while only 6 percent of the total raised by challengers came from PACs.[62] In California, in the eighteen-month period that ended June 30, 1990, only 3 percent of the donations from the twenty-five largest business-related PACs went to legislative candidates challenging an incumbent.[63]

This pattern is fueling the growing disparity between the campaign cash available to incumbents and challengers. In 1976, incumbents in the California Assembly were outspending challengers by 3-to-1 in general elections. By 1984, this ratio had increased to 14-to-1. In 1986, it doubled to 30-to-1. The imbalance was even greater in the California Senate: the fund-raising advantage of incumbents over challengers was a staggering 62-to-1 in 1986.[64] The fund-raising advantage of incumbency increases even further when primary elections are taken into account. The bottom line is that not a single incumbent was defeated for reelection to the California legislature in 1986,[65] nor to the California Senate in 1988.

The lopsided fund-raising ratio is explained in part by the increasing tendency of state legislators to follow their congressional counterparts in raising money in off years. In 1985 in California, virtually all off-year contributions went to incumbents, and more than 85 percent of this type of money was provided by PACs, business entities, and labor organizations.[66]

As goes California, so goes the nation. Just as the California Commission on Campaign Financing found an 8 percent drop between 1984 and 1986 in the number of candidates seeking legislative office, Gary Moncrief's study found a drop in candidates for six of the eight legislative chambers in Montana, Idaho, Washington, and Oregon during the 1980–88 period. "In several cases the decline is precipitous," he writes,[67] adding, "The data are quite consistent in revealing a growing incumbent advantage in spending."[68]

The problem is succinctly framed by Ruth Jones in her review of state-level campaign finance reform in the 1980s: ". . . when campaign costs sky rocket, and wealthy special interests fund certain categories of candidates (usually incumbents) but not others, when qualified candidates refuse to run for election because they fear they cannot effectively compete for campaign resources, when those in power can preempt potential challengers through the accumulation of great campaign war chests—when those circumstances develop the ideal of democratic elections is severely challenged."[69]

# Chapter 2

# The Good, the Bad, and
# the Unforeseen

State capitals across the country—Sacramento, Phoenix, Columbia, Trenton—are rife with complaints, on and off the record, of lobbyists and PAC managers being threatened with adverse legislative action for failure to make sizable campaign contributions. New Jersey offers an interesting case study because—notwithstanding a sometimes sordid political past—the state has held itself up to national scrutiny in recent years as a model of campaign finance reform.

On September 21, 1989, barely six weeks before the biennial elections for the New Jersey Assembly, four of the Assembly's top Democrats held a meeting with a lobbyist representing one of the state capital's best-funded political action committees, Lawyers Encouraging Government and Law (LEGAL). Such sessions are not unusual these days in any of the fifty state capitals. With PACs providing an ever-greater share of the funding for state legislative candidates—PAC contributions in the 1987 contest for the New Jersey legislature more than doubled over four years earlier[1]—the Democrats were relying on this type of donation to help them to regain majority control of the Assembly.

But Karen Kotvas, the lobbyist for LEGAL, later told a reporter for the Bergen *Record* that the Democrats had not merely requested a contribution from her group. The meeting, she said, had amounted to a "shakedown."[2]

LEGAL already was a major benefactor of the state Democratic party; during the 1989 campaign, it contributed almost $90,000 directly to the party's candidates. But, as Kotvas tells it, four Assembly leaders—Joseph Doria, John Paul Doyle, Willie Brown, and Wayne Bryant—had their own legislative PAC, the "Democratic Assembly Majority," with a fund-raising goal of $200,000.[3] Kotvas said that Doyle had told her

LEGAL's "share" was $20,000, and that Brown had warned that a failure to ante up could result in bills important to LEGAL not being "posted," or considered, in the forthcoming legislative session.[4]

The four Democrats have denied heatedly that they requested any specific contribution or that they made any threats. Bryant, who became the Assembly majority leader after the Democrats took control in the November 1989 election, said that about two dozen lobbyists were invited to a series of strategy sessions held over a period of three days. "We asked them for their financial help as well as their input," he said.[5] As of early 1991, no charges had been filed in the matter, although the allegations remained "under review," according to the director of the New Jersey Division of Criminal Justice.[6]

Ironically, there was one point on which Kotvas and Doria, now the Assembly speaker, concurred: the offensiveness of the current system by which New Jersey legislative candidates raise campaign funds. Declared Kotvas, "We're all victims of a system that is obscene, out of control and forces legislators to raise this kind of money." Doria agreed, "There is no question the amount of money spent on legislative elections is obscene."[7]

The New Jersey legislature passed a sweeping financial disclosure statute in 1973 and, a year later, became the first state to enact a comprehensive program for partial public funding of gubernatorial general elections. In 1980, that system was extended to cover gubernatorial primaries as well. Consequently, New Jersey has achieved the desirable goal of opening the electoral arena to those with limited resources while curtailing the flow of special interest money into the governorship race.

However, in the two decades since enacting public funding for gubernatorial candidates, the legislature has not extended the system to its own electoral contests. In fact, there is not even a limit on the amounts that can be given to legislative candidates by an individual, PAC, union, or most corporations. This contrasts with Minnesota and Wisconsin, which both publicly fund state legislative as well as statewide offices. The inevitable result has been an upward spiral of spending for New Jersey Senate and Assembly contests, increasing the pressure to collect more and more donations.

If there is a final irony in the New Jersey story, it is that these pressures have been accelerated by the system of gubernatorial public funding. As at the federal level—where presidential public funding has encouraged PACs to turn their attention to congressional races—the restrictions on participation by interest groups in the New Jersey gubernatorial race, far from eliminating this type of political money, have simply redirected it through other available channels. The legislature is a natural target of those with money to make political contributions.

Possible solutions to New Jersey's wide-open system of campaign financing in state legislative elections were being considered in 1991—as members of the legislature sought to reassure voters that they were serious about public ethics and governmental integrity following the Kotvas affair and a 1990 grand jury investigation into allegations of wrongdoing by legislative staffers. (No indictments were returned.) A study group appointed by New Jersey legislative leaders recommended that the current campaign finance regulatory structure be tightened. However, the group, whose findings will be discussed in detail later, did not recommend public financing of legislative campaigns.

## The New Politics of New Jersey

Unlike such states as Minnesota and Wisconsin, whose systems of public financing emerged from a tradition of progressive politics and clean campaigns, New Jersey's experiment was in part an effort to get out from under its reputation as one of the more corrupt states in the country.

Longtime New Jersey political observers say the reform movement picked up steam a generation ago when an official in the Hudson County (which includes Jersey City) Democratic organization admitted publicly what was already widely suspected—that the state's urban political machines ran largely on assessments from holders of patronage jobs and kickbacks from contractors. "We go to the guys who have contracts with the county, and if they don't contribute, business isn't as good next year," one crony of Hudson County Democratic boss John V. Kenny is reported to have declared.[8]

Kenny and eight associates, including Jersey City's mayor and city council president, were indicted in 1970 on charges of conspiracy and extortion. Kenny was severed from the trial due to ill health, but the other eight were convicted a year later of taking $3.3 million in kickbacks.[9] This was but one of several highly publicized corruption trials in New Jersey in the early 1970s. In several instances, the indictments reached into the highest levels of state government. Within the space of little more than a year, New Jersey had the unenviable distinction of seeing two secretaries of state and two state treasurers convicted or plead guilty to corruption charges relating to campaign finance abuses.[10]

Responding to widespread voter concern about corruption, the Democrats in 1973 nominated a candidate for governor who, while virtually unknown statewide, had earned a reputation for unquestioned integrity. He was Brendan Byrne, a judge and former prosecutor in Essex County. Three years earlier, federal prosecutors had released wiretapped conversations of a mob figure named Angelo "Gyp" DeCarlo. The tapes were full of references to New Jersey politicians whom the mob believed to be on the take. But when it came to Byrne, DeCarlo had declared, "It's Byrne, we can't make him"—meaning Byrne could not be bribed. Another voice on the tape then chimed in, "What's wrong with Byrne, doesn't he like money?"[11]

Elected by a landslide, Byrne took advantage of his mandate to push through a public financing amendment to the 1973 Campaign Contributions and Reporting Act, a law passed during the administration of Byrne's predecessor, Republican William Cahill. In April 1974, six months before the current system of public financing of presidential elections was enacted by Congress, the New Jersey legislature approved public funding of future gubernatorial elections. In 1977, the state held the nation's first publicly funded gubernatorial race, in which Byrne won reelection. Public funding was extended to gubernatorial primaries as well in 1980.

### The "Presidentialized" Governor's Race

"All signs indicate that New Jersey's Public Financing Program has succeeded in allowing persons of limited means to run for governor and in eliminating undue influence from gubernatorial campaigns," the New Jersey Election Law Enforcement Commission (ELEC) wrote in 1986, shortly after the state's third publicly financed contest had been held.[12]

But there also have been some unintended, and not always salutary, side effects—not only in New Jersey, but in several other states that have adopted public financing programs in recent years. In the same report in which it praised the operation of the New Jersey system, ELEC reiterated its call for doing away with overall expenditure limits on the grounds that they disadvantage nonincumbents.[13]

In addition, just as state legislative contests around the country have become "congressionalized," the New Jersey governor's race shows signs of becoming "presidentialized." Spending limits in the publicly financed race for the presidency have been circumvented by use of independent expenditures and "soft money"; now these less than desirable forms of political money have begun to make an appearance in New Jersey. "The commission believes that the effect of expenditure limits may be to encourage circumvention of the expenditure and contribution limits by independent expenditures," ELEC said in its 1986 report.[14]

New Jersey's system of public financing is arguably the most generous in the country. After reaching an initial threshold of $150,000 in fundraising (which was only $50,000 until increased in 1989 by the legislature), a candidate is eligible to receive two dollars in public funding for every dollar raised, up to a specified ceiling. In return, he or she must abide by limits on individual contributions as well as overall expenditures and agree to participate in two debates in the primary and two in the general election.

In the past, questions were raised as to whether this scheme was so generous that it produced more electoral competition than New Jersey voters could have wanted—or needed. In 1981, the first year in which public financing was extended to the gubernatorial primary, a total of sixteen candidates received public funds in the two party primaries. With Byrne barred by statute from seeking a third term, the prospect of not having to run against a sitting incumbent made the race desirable to many aspirants. Critics complained that public money was being wasted on an overabundance of office seekers; some even argued that public funding itself was responsible for attracting some candidates into the race.

This criticism was muted when the winner of the 1981 general election, Republican Thomas Kean, sought another term in 1985. With Kean enjoying immense popularity, only six candidates—Kean and five Democrats—sought public funding. When Kean's second term expired, leaving an open seat in 1989, eight candidates qualified for public financing, only half the number of the 1981 free-for-all.

All told, over four election cycles, of the forty major candidates who have sought the governorship since public funding was enacted in New Jersey, thirty-eight have sought and received the subsidies.[15] Advocates say this rate of participation stands as evidence that the system is working. They contrast New Jersey with several other states where the public money available to candidates is so minimal that it is not worth their while to participate in the system and abide by the related spending limits.

In addition, data from recent campaigns appear to substantiate ELEC's claim that the New Jersey system has sharply limited the effect of special interest groups and wealthy individuals in gubernatorial races. These individuals and groups may donate no more than $1,500 to a candidate (this limit was raised from $800 in 1989).

The large donor has by no means disappeared. In the 1985 general election campaign, much of the money raised privately by Kean and Democratic challenger Peter Shapiro came from contributions of $600 or more.[16] What is significant is that Kean's and Shapiro's private donations represented only about 40 percent of their overall campaign budgets in the general election; the remaining 60 percent came from public funds. Likewise, in the gubernatorial primary more than 58 percent of campaign spending was underwritten by public financing.[17]

The pattern in the 1989 election, in which Democrat James Florio beat Republican James Courter, was similar. In the primary, 58 percent of the expenses were met by public funds, the same proportion as four years earlier.[18] During the general election, in which Florio and Courter each reported spending a bit less than the generous ceiling of $5 million, each received $3.3 million in public funds—the maximum permitted by law.

However, questions are being raised as to whether these overall spending ceilings are merely illusory, and whether using the lure of public funding to induce compliance is in fact workable.

### Punching a Hole in the Ceiling

In 1988, Republican George Bush and Democrat Michael Dukakis were officially limited to spending $54.4 million each in the presidential general election race, with all but about $8 million of that coming from public funds. In reality, $106.5 million was spent by or on behalf of Dukakis, and $93.7 million by or on behalf of Bush.[19] "Soft money" accounted for most of the difference between the official limits and the actual spending. Much of this soft money was raised by Bush and Dukakis campaign officials but funneled through state and local parties, a procedure legitimized by Congress in 1979.

Likewise, the rise of soft money in the New Jersey gubernatorial race can be attributed to a change in campaign finance laws and regulations and the inventiveness of candidates and their operatives to find new channels for funding. They want to win any way they can, and so they help to raise money for party committees to spend. These pressures demonstrate the difficulties in trying to regulate money strictly in the American political arena, be it at the state or federal level.

It is, at best, daunting to attempt to restrain legislators from voting to make life easier for themselves, particularly when they perceive their own or their party's political survival to be at stake. It is altogether impossible to prevent a savvy election lawyer from finding a hole in expenditure ceilings wide enough to drive a campaign message through.

Bob Fitzpatrick, a fellow at Rutgers University's Eagleton Institute of Politics, notes, "Since 1974, [New Jersey] policymakers have protected and expanded the role of political parties. Some critics have contended . . .

that this has fostered the development of creative mechanisms for bypassing the existing limits on gubernatorial campaign spending by creating organizations which funnel money in ways that benefit the candidates.

"Without a doubt, the state parties today have become surrogate fundraisers and surrogate spenders for the gubernatorial candidates," he adds.[20]

Under New Jersey law, each county political organization is limited to spending $10,000 on behalf of a gubernatorial candidate, yielding a total of $210,000 for the state's twenty-one counties. However, the state Democratic and Republican parties, as well as their affiliated legislative leadership committees, while directing most of their efforts toward legislative candidates, in recent years have produced "generic" advertising in the form of costly television commercials. These soft money campaigns were widely viewed as an effort to boost the gubernatorial candidates, whose own advertising budgets are restricted by the expenditure limits that accompany acceptance of public funding.

The first widespread use of this tactic came in 1981, when Kean defeated Florio in the closest gubernatorial contest in state history. Drawing heavily on help from the well-funded Republican National Committee, the New Jersey GOP was able to allocate about $800,000 for so-called institutional advertising— about twice what the Democrats spent.[21] All told, the state Republican party spent more than $1.5 million on advertising and get-out-the-vote efforts above and beyond the $2.1 million official ceiling imposed on Kean's general election effort that year. In the 1985 election, Kean and the Republican party outspent the Democrats again; this time Kean was the incumbent, and fund-raising was easier.

Florio and the Democrats clearly learned a lesson from those experiences. Roger Bodman, who managed Kean's 1981 race, estimates that Florio and the Democrats had combined expenditures of about $15 million in 1989, well in excess of the $5 million officially spent by Florio in the general election. That is almost twice as much as the $8 million that Bodman figures was spent by Courter and the Republicans.[22] While Democratic estimates are lower, there is no question that party spending has become substantial.

Changes made prior to the 1989 election helped to spur this type of spending. In revising the state's public funding regulations, ELEC allowed political party organizations and individual candidates to produce literature, bumper stickers, and other material using the name or picture of that party's gubernatorial candidate. (Congress took similar action a decade earlier in its soft money provision.) Also permitted in the 1989 revisions was the use of the gubernatorial nominee's name in direct mail and telephone efforts run by party organizations or local candidates.

"To anyone other than the seasoned operative . . . these may seem like relatively minor amendments to New Jersey's campaign finance system," Fitzpatrick writes. "In fact, they represent a significant departure from past practice—and their effect has been to revolutionize the way in which both parties, and their gubernatorial candidates, run and finance their campaigns."[23]

Such revisions undermine contribution limits as well as expenditure ceilings. At the federal level, there are strict limits on how much an individual may contribute to a presidential candidate or a national party committee. There are no limits, however, to the amount that an individual may give to a state or local party committee. Consequently, 267 individuals were able to give soft money donations of $100,000 or more in 1988 to aid Bush, and 130 individuals gave similar amounts in an effort to help Dukakis.

In New Jersey, while an individual or PAC now may give no more than $1,500 to a gubernatorial candidate, there are no limits when it comes to contributions to a political party; the party spending limits apply only to direct expenditures on behalf of the candidates, such as television advertising.

"The historic norm in the U.S. has been to view parties as quasi-private organizations and to restrain government involvement (including regulation) in the activities of legally recognized political parties," Ruth Jones writes. "In the 1980s, however, parties are increasingly caught in the crosswinds between those who seek to continue the tradition of autonomous and independent political parties and those who see the reemergence of party organizations as a threat to existing as well as future legislation to control campaign contributions and expenditures."[24]

Compounding the soft money explosion is that of independent expenditures, in which an individual or group mounts an advertising effort without the candidate's knowledge or consent. Restrictions on this kind of campaigning were ruled unconstitutional by the U.S. Supreme Court in its landmark *Buckley v. Valeo* decision of 1976, as long as there is no coordination between a candidate and an independent expenditure effort. This device gained prominence in the federal elections of 1980, when several conservative groups spent millions in an effort to elect Ronald Reagan and defeat several liberal Democratic senators. Independent expenditure campaigns arouse controversy because they have generally been used to try to defeat rather than elect a candidate, accompanied often by sharply negative ads.

If states have frequently served as laboratories—and prods—for reform at the federal level, both independent expenditures and soft money represent instances in which forms of political finance activity originating in federal campaigns are seeping down to the state level.

A year after their first widespread appearance at the federal level, independent expenditure campaigns surfaced repeatedly during the 1981 gubernatorial race in New Jersey.[25] One controversial case involved the National Rifle Association (NRA), which mailed letters to about 50,000 of its New Jersey members urging support to Florio in the Democratic primary.[26] Two of Florio's principal opponents filed complaints with ELEC, arguing that the NRA's mailing violated an $800 contribution limit then in force for individuals and corporations. Florio campaign officials countered that they did not know of the mailing in advance and in no way participated in it. ELEC, after an investigation, dismissed the complaint.

In 1985, in a case involving two New Jersey Republican legislative candidates who engaged in joint advertising with Kean, ELEC took the position that 15 percent of the cost of the ads represented a contribution to Kean and had to be charged against his spending ceiling. Both Kean and the legislative candidates took the matter to court, saying that—because the Kean campaign had no knowledge of the joint ads and had not consented to them—they amounted to independent spending. The matter ultimately reached the New Jersey supreme court, which decided against ELEC and in favor of Kean.[27]

In 1989, Republicans were unsuccessful in contending that an independent advertising campaign in favor of abortion rights should be counted against Florio's spending limit. ELEC never received a written complaint and was never provided with proof that the effort, underwritten by the National Organization for Women, had been coordinated with Florio or his campaign.[28]

### Putting a Lid on the Challenger

Efforts to loosen the strictures of the expenditure limits date back to New Jersey's first publicly funded gubernatorial race in 1977, when Governor Byrne faced a stiff challenge from Republican state senator Raymond Bateman. That race illustrates the difficulties inherent in the expenditure ceiling issue: while such limits are tough to enforce, strict adherence to them can work to the detriment of a candidate without widespread name recognition.

In 1977, the general election ceiling for spending was $1.5 million for each gubernatorial nominee. This was a relatively low limit given New Jersey's demographic realities. While it is small and the nation's most densely populated state, it is sandwiched between New York and Pennsylvania, with much of its population living in the New York City and Philadelphia media markets. Advertising time in either of these markets is among the most expensive in the country. (One prominent political consultant, Robert Squier, has dubbed New Jersey's public funding program "the Philadelphia and New York Broadcasters' Relief Act.")[29]

Bateman, less well known than his incumbent opponent, found himself sandwiched between high costs and a low spending cap late in the 1977 campaign. In a report issued later, ELEC wrote, "As public support for the candidates shifted toward Governor Byrne, Senator Bateman, solely because of the expenditure limit, was unable to react and mount an alternative campaign to counteract the growth of support for Governor Byrne."[30]

Bateman had started the campaign with a significant advantage. Notwithstanding his landslide election in 1973, Governor Byrne had suffered through a bumpy transition in his introduction to the statewide political arena. He was widely accused of failing to keep his fences mended. But his largest political problem was that he had pushed a state income tax through the legislature in response to a court decision on statewide funding for education—a switch from his statements during the 1973 race that such a levy would not be needed.

In part, Byrne's victory in the June 1977 primary was the result of his opposition being split among nine different candidates. Early general election polls showed him as a ten-point underdog to Bateman (who had handily won the Republican primary against Kean, then making his first run for governor). But the polls showed Bateman's lead to be less the result of support for the Republican than of opposition to Byrne. Consequently, Bateman faced the expensive task of carving out a clear identification among the voters.

Throughout the summer, he sought to solidify his image—with limited success. Polls indicated that opposition to an income tax was abating. The public came to be skeptical that an alternative plan put forth by Bateman could prevent serious cuts in state services. The political momentum began to move in the direction of the incumbent.

It was in this context that the Republican State Committee sought funding for an anti-Byrne television campaign. In what was to be the first of many efforts to circumvent the spending ceilings in the gubernatorial race, the Republicans sent out a fund-raising letter that read: "You can help Ray [Bateman] beyond the $600 [individual contribution] limit by supporting Republican legislative candidates."[31]

The Byrne campaign promptly filed a complaint with ELEC, charging that the television campaign violated the spending limits of the governorship race. ELEC ruled that the Republican fund-raising appeal did not violate the law, in that the money was not solicited by or for the Bateman campaign itself. However, ELEC ruled that Bateman had benefited from the anti-Byrne television campaign, and said that two-thirds of the cost of the commericals had to be charged against Bateman's spending limit.[32]

The ruling came barely two weeks prior to Election Day, with both the Byrne and Bateman campaigns approaching the spending ceiling. As the commission later noted:

> Both campaigns were compelled to reimburse their respective political party committees and were unable to make other planned expenditures during the week before the election.
>
> Between the two candidates, Governor Byrne and Senator Bateman, the latter was more seriously hurt by the reallocation because his campaign committee had to shift more than $70,000 from planned expenditures to the Republican State Committee shortly before the election.[33]

The problems encountered by Bateman led ELEC to call for a repeal of the expenditure limits, a recommendation that it repeated after both the 1981 and 1985 gubernatorial contests. In its 1986 report, the commission argued that expenditure limits put nonincumbents at a disadvantage and encourage independent expenditure efforts. More fundamentally, "The expenditure limits unnecessarily restrict first amendment rights of free speech and deny a candidate the opportunity to demonstrate widespread support among less wealthy voters by attracting as many small contributors as possible."[34]

ELEC suggested a scheme commonly known as "floors without ceilings." While recommending that candidates not be held to an expenditure limit, the commission proposed a new formula under which gubernatorial aspirants would be eligible for up to $500,000 in public funding in the primary and $1 million in the general election. In a floors-without-ceilings approach, candidates are given enough public funding to help get their message across to the voters without an excessive reliance on large contributors and special interest money, but they can spend unlimited amounts.

Three years after the Bateman–Byrne race, in 1980, the New Jersey legislature voted to do away with expenditure ceilings. But Governor Byrne, who had benefited from them, vetoed the measure. Almost a decade later, in 1989, the legislature acted to mitigate the problems caused by a low spending limit. It raised the general election ceiling by 125 percent (from $2.2 million to $5 million), while doubling the expenditure limit in the primary (from $1.1 million to $2.2 million). The legislature also adopted a system to provide automatic, inflation-adjusted increases for the spending ceilings as well as for contribution limits and amounts of public funding available to candidates.

The legislature's action boosted the total cost of the 1989 New Jersey gubernatorial race to more than $25 million for the primary and general elections combined, with more than $15 million of that coming from public funds. That is almost two and a half times the $10.5 million spent in 1985 (an election that admittedly pitted a popular incumbent against a lesser-known challenger), underscoring the difficulty of simultaneously holding down total spending and ensuring competitive elections.

## Public Funding and Legislative Elections

While spending in the New Jersey gubernatorial contest has jumped because the legislature raised the limits and the funding, the tremendous spending races in the legislators' own contests are strictly the product of a free market: no expenditure ceilings, no contribution limits, and no public financing.

In 1987, candidates for the New Jersey state Senate and Assembly spent $11.5 million, an almost threefold increase from the $3.9 million spent a decade earlier.[35] Even more striking is the increase in six-figure contests. In 1977, no legislative candidate spent more than $100,000. In 1981, only two state Senate candidates reached that level. But, in 1987, twenty-nine candidates (twenty-three state Senate aspirants and six Assembly hopefuls) exceeded $100,000; two of them spent more than $300,000 apiece.[36]

An even sharper increase occurred in the total amounts raised by legislative candidates, which jumped from $4.1 million in 1977 to $14.8 million in 1987.[37] As in so many other states, this trend has worked to the clear advantage of incumbents, who received 63 percent of the funds collected in 1987. Not surprisingly, 98 percent were returned to office.[38]

PACs and other lobbying interests have turned their attention to legislative contests as the strictures of the publicly funded governor's race have limited their clout in that forum. The New Jersey Election Law Enforcement Commission remarked, "While the special interest PACs were not, by themselves, the driving force behind the increase in legislative campaign spending in 1987, it can be said that special interests in general, including business and union contributors, were the major factor in the financial activities of legislative candidates in 1987."[39] The commission also noted that a third of the money going to legislative candidates had come directly from PACs, businesses, and unions. "This trend in PAC activity, barring statutory change, is likely to grow and develop further in future years, with PAC momentum growing unabated until political action committees are clearly pinpointed as the driving force behind future increases in legislative campaign financial activity."

ELEC's study also showed a notable rise in so-called officeholder or leadership PACs, by which New Jersey legislative leaders solicit funds from lobbyists and then collect chits by distributing the money to needy candidates. In 1983, there were only three such officeholder PACs, and they raised a relatively modest total of $130,000. By 1987, there were seventy-eight—a 2,500 percent increase from four years earlier—which collected more than $2.3 million.[40]

The image of a legislature receiving and spending more and more money has spurred the frequency of calls for reform. In early 1988, midway through his second term, Governor Kean urged legislators to "take a look at ways to put the brakes on the soaring costs of legislative campaigns."[41] A year later, Kean, a Republican, asked the legislature to consider public financing of legislative elections. "The legislature has changed a great deal. . . . Members spend more and more time raising money and less time dealing with substantive issues. Gone are the homemakers, small storeowners or community activists.

"We are very close to the day when the only candidates for the state legislature will be the wealthy lawyers or fulltime politicians," he continued. "Public service should not be a pastime or vocation for the privileged few."[42]

In July 1989, ELEC lent its support to the concept of public financing without endorsing any specific proposal. "Legislative public financing would provide a means for candidates to raise the money they need to conduct effective campaigns, and at the same time reduce the possibility of corruption," the commission wrote. "It would help to increase public trust in the electoral process and in government, increase voter participation, enable candidates of limited means to run for the Assembly or the Senate, and let candidates spend more time campaigning."[43]

However, the prospects for enactment of public financing of legislative elections in New Jersey appear dim. The Ad Hoc Commission on Legislative Ethics and Campaign Finance, established by legislative leaders in the Spring of 1990, issued its findings the following October. The group recommended against public funding of legislative elections, saying a majority of its members had concluded that "this alternative to the current system of campaign finance would not curb the costs of elections, limit the potential influence of large donors or level the playing field among candidates."[44]

The Ad Hoc Commission cited the potential cost of the proposal— $5 million to $10 million, depending on whether it was a year in which both the state Senate and Assembly were up for reelection—"at a time when the state was facing a serious budget crisis, a shortfall in revenues and little support for increased taxes."[45]

The commission did, however, propose extending to legislative races the $1,500 contribution limit now imposed on individuals, PACs, businesses, and unions that choose to get involved in the governor's race. It also recommended a $25,000 per year limit on the amount any individual or entity can give to a state party or a legislative leadership committee/officeholder PAC. The commission said it "makes this recommendation with the hope of ending the proliferation of this type of committee while at the same time strengthening the ability of party leaders in the legislature to help elect or reelect party candidates."[46]

The fate of these proposals now rests with the legislature.

## Beyond New Jersey: The State of State Public Funding

New Jersey legislators may be reluctant—for reasons political as well as budgetary—to impose public financing upon themselves. But they have not been hesitant to appropriate public funding for the gubernatorial race. In the four elections since 1977, the legislature has provided $32.2 million in subsidies to those seeking the governorship, with $15.2 million furnished in 1989 alone. No other state comes close to that mark.

Including New Jersey, there are now twenty-two states that have some form of direct public funding of elections on the books.[47] What is impressive is that, during the past five years, a half dozen states have passed public financing programs while Congress has been stalemated as to whether to extend such a system to contests for the House and Senate. The bad news is that all but a handful of these state programs have had limited success in attracting tax checkoff money, candidate acceptance, or both (see Figure 3).

**Figure 3**
A Problem for Public Funding:
Less Support for Tax Checkoffs

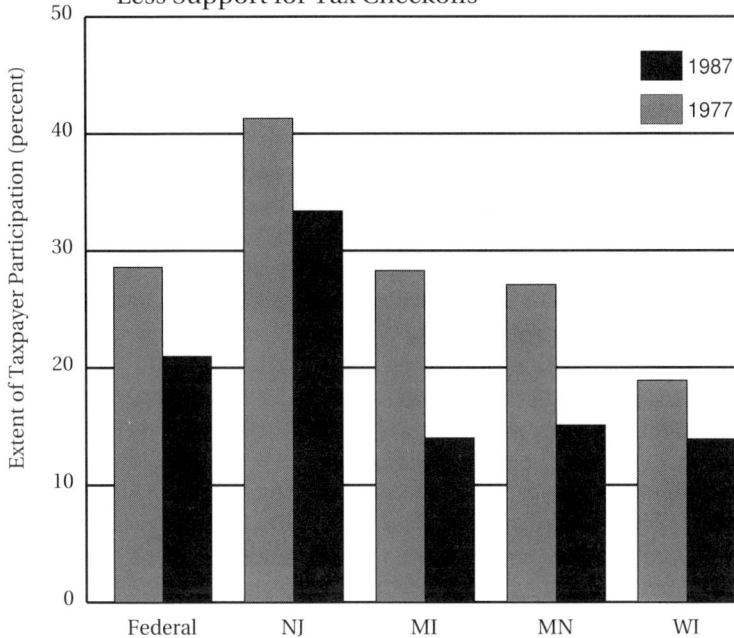

Sources: Compiled from Federal Election Commission and
Citizens' Research Foundation.

As will be discussed in Chapter 3, two states, Florida and Maryland, enacted programs but retreated from their implementation. In 1991, Florida reenacted its program. Indiana has an unusual setup by which revenue from the sale of personalized license plates goes to state and county party committees. This system, a throwback to the days when profits from local motor vehicle bureaus went to support the political party that controlled the governorship, has proved to be controversial.

In late 1989, however, the Republican state chairman announced he was returning about $200,000 in so-called PLP revenues to the state. His move was triggered, at least in part, by fears that continued acceptance of the money would bring the state Republican party under the coverage of Indiana's open records law, thereby subjecting the GOP to an audit. The state Democratic party subsequently announced that it, too, would forgo PLP revenue. Despite the position of the two state parties, some county committees continued to accept the money. A move to replace the PLP system with a $1 income tax checkoff failed during the 1990 legislative session—due largely to lobbying by the powerful Marion County (includes Indianapolis) Republican organization, which wanted to maintain the status quo. Then a change in state party leaderships led both parties to resume acceptance of the money—and the audits that go with it. The money proved more powerful than the principle.

That leaves twenty states that currently depend on the state income tax system to raise money for public funding of campaigns. But eight of these rely entirely on tax "add-ons," in which a taxpayer may donate anywhere from one to twenty-five dollars, depending on the state. The problem is that, because this increases one's tax liability, participation in such programs is minimal. In no state do more than 2 percent of the taxpayers choose to add on, and the average rate in 1988 was 0.7 percent.

The result is a paltry amount available to either a candidate or political party, depending on the manner in which a state legislature has decided to allocate the money. In Virginia, for example, the add-on raised less than $50,000 in 1988 for party organizations. Contrast this with the more than $25 million spent on that state's gubernatorial race alone in 1989. In Maine and Alabama, where the money also goes to a political party designated by the taxpayer, the take from the add-on was a mere $17,200 and $15,100, respectively.

The campaign add-on is frequently competing against other programs listed on the state income tax form, thereby further undermining potential revenues. "In several states, political campaign add-on programs are listed alongside other add-on programs designed to assist the arts, to protect the environment, or to prevent child abuse," notes Ruth Jones. "This suggests that, along with many other topics, campaign financing is perceived as a worthwhile 'cause' rather than as a fundamental component of democratic elections."[48] Since Colorado set up a wildlife add-on in the mid-1970s, some forty-eight states have adopted environmental add-ons for protecting animals, plants, or wetlands.[49]

The remaining twelve states with public financing, including New Jersey, have tax checkoffs. Again, depending on the state, the taxpayer may dedicate one to five dollars to public financing of elections. Like the dollar checkoff on federal tax returns, this does not increase a taxpayer's overall liability. Therefore, it is more popular and raises substantially more money than the add-on option. In 1988, the average checkoff rate was 16 percent.

However, the campaign checkoff also faces increasing competition from add-ons. In Michigan, the decline in designations to the state campaign fund became more pronounced in the early 1980s after competing add-ons were added to fund programs for children and wildlife. These funds have been more extensively publicized than the campaign fund; there is a feeling that many taxpayers still do not realize that the checkoff neither decreases a taxpayer's refund nor increases his or her tax liability.[50] Probably many people are cynical about the electoral process and feel that one dollar from them will not make a difference.

New Jersey is exceptional in that nearly 33 percent of the taxpayers participate in the one-dollar campaign checkoff. And, unlike the other checkoff states, the money does not go directly into a separate fund dedicated to campaign financing. Rather, the money that has financed the New Jersey gubernatorial election comes from legislative appropriations, reimbursed by the checkoff funds, and the legislature has frequently appropriated more funding than has been collected through the checkoff.

In contrast, most other states have checkoff participation rates ranging from one-half to barely one-quarter of New Jersey's, and must live within the means provided by the checkoff funding. In Michigan, if the checkoff raises an amount insufficient to provide candidates with their full allocation of public funding, the subsidy is proportionately reduced. In Wisconsin, where the public financing program extends even to nonpartisan candidates such as state superintendent of instruction and supreme court justices, the decline in the tax checkoff has jeopardized the program beyond 1992.

Of the twelve states with checkoffs, eight either provide the funding exclusively to political parties or divide it among political parties and candidates (see Appendix 1). This tends to diffuse the impact on—and benefit to—candidates seeking "seed" money to mount a viable campaign. There are four states that allocate all of the money directly to candidates: New Jersey, Michigan, Wisconsin, and Hawaii; Minnesota, Rhode Island, and North Carolina provide for both selected candidates and parties.

Under the 1976 Supreme Court decision in *Buckley v. Valeo*, a candidate cannot be forced to campaign within an expenditure limit. But he or she may volunteer to do so in return for a benefit, such as public financing. As a practical matter, this means that public funding programs—at the federal, state, and local levels—must offer a candidate enough money to make it worthwhile to accept a spending limit. Clearly, the high rate of candidate participation in the New Jersey program is evidence that the quantity of public funding there has outweighed the restrictions of spending limits in the perception of most gubernatorial aspirants.

In Hawaii, however, nonfederal candidates were for many years given a mere $50 per election, primary and general ($100 per election year), in subsidies in return for abiding by spending limits. In 1984, a grand total of two legislative candidates took the state up on this less than enticing offer. The number of participating candidates crept up to three in 1986 and five in 1988. However, in a move that applied only to the 1990 elections, the legislature raised the public funding grant to $250 per election and $500 per election year; the results were dramatic as eighteen legislative candidates accepted the public funding.

Consequently, Michigan, Minnesota, and Wisconsin are the states apart from New Jersey that have a history of providing substantial financial assistance to candidates. Michigan, like New Jersey, limits public funding to the gubernatorial contest. Also like New Jersey, the public funding has been at a level sufficient to attract widespread candidate acceptance. From 1978 through the 1990 elections, twenty-one of twenty-three Michigan gubernatorial aspirants opted to take public funding and abide by spending limits; one exception was a millionaire who ran a largely self-financed (and unsuccessful) campaign in the 1986 Republican primary,[51] and the other ran in the 1990 Republican primary.

In Minnesota, where all statewide office seekers are eligible for public financing in the general election, it appears that the system has encouraged competition. No one has run for statewide office unchallenged since the law was enacted, and the number of legislators running unopposed has decreased.[52]

### Legislative Public Funding: Has It Worked?

Minnesota and Wisconsin are the only states that provide significant public financing of legislative elections along the lines of the proposals now under debate in New Jersey. In both states, however, the funding is limited to the general election. Candidate participation in these programs, which has generally been high, has ebbed and flowed with the amount of public subsidy available. But some critics question whether the plans have achieved their goal of restraining costs and increasing competition.

In Minnesota, candidates receive funding allocations based on a complicated formula that takes into account the right of a taxpayer to designate which party's candidates he or she wants to assist. In the 1988 contests for the Minnesota House, candidates participating in the program were limited to expenditures of $18,597; the average public funding allotment was $4,588, or about one-quarter of the spending ceiling. In the 1986 legislative elections in Wisconsin, state Senate candidates were limited to spending $34,500 and received $15,525 each in public funding, 45 percent of the general election limit.[53] Wisconsin's program has served to curtail PAC contributions through a provision that reduces the amount of a candidate's public subsidy by the amount of PAC donations received.

In 1980, when members of both the Minnesota House and Senate were up for election, the rate of candidate participation in the program declined to 66 percent from 92 percent only four years earlier. At the time, with annual inflation running into double digits, neither the expenditure limits nor the amount of public grant had been raised to take that into account. Thus, public money was insufficient to be attractive to some candidates.

After the 1980 election, both spending limits and public fund allocations were tied to the consumer price index. In 1990, participation among Minnesota legislative candidates was back up to 92 percent, although this includes office seekers who signed onto the system but did not make it through the primary and therefore could not take advantage of the money.[54] Since government cannot compel spending limits, and since the appeal of taxpayer subsidies rises roughly in proportion to their real value, it appears that public financing cannot effectively brake campaign spending.

A similar problem has occurred in Wisconsin in recent years, as money raised from the one-dollar tax checkoff has declined. Public funding grants fell from $15,525 in 1986 to $13,630 in 1988 for state Senate candidates and from $7,763 to $6,355 for Assembly contenders. This had the effect of dropping public funding from about 45 percent to less than 40 percent of the overall spending ceiling. Consequently, while three-quarters of the candidates for legislature participated in the program in 1986, fewer than two-thirds of those running opted to do so in 1988.

In an effort to mitigate the problem, the Democratic-controlled legislature voted to increase the checkoff to two dollars in 1988 and again in 1989. In both instances, the move was vetoed by the state's Republican governor. Such incidents highlight the ideological differences between Democrats and Republicans over public funding, and raise questions as to whether it may benefit one party over another.

In states where the money goes into a single fund and is awarded without regard to partisan affiliation, many Republicans clearly have seen it in their self-interest to accept the funding—philosophical reservations notwithstanding. Among the states with major public funding programs, only Minnesota allocates some of the money based on a taxpayer's partisan choice. In 1980, Minnesota Democratic candidates were outdistancing their Republican counterparts by 69 percent to 31 percent in the distribution of public funds, due both to a greater number of

Democratic-leaning tax filers and the greater willingness of Democratic candidates to accept the money. However, that gap had narrowed to 54–46 by 1984, and it stood at 57–43 in 1988.

More significant than the Democrat versus Republican issue is that of incumbent versus challenger. There is mixed evidence as to how much legislative public financing has "leveled the playing field" and reduced the tremendous name recognition and fund-raising advantages enjoyed by incumbents.

In both Minnesota and Wisconsin, some encouraging trends have emerged with regard to legislative elections. Fewer incumbents are running unopposed, and the challenger share of total election spending is significantly higher than in other states. In Wisconsin, challengers actually have received a greater proportion of public funding than incumbents during recent elections.[55]

However, in rejecting legislative public funding for New Jersey, the Ad Hoc Commission on Legislative Ethics and Campaign Finance found that the Minnesota and Wisconsin programs were "not working entirely as intended," and that they tended to benefit incumbents rather than challengers. The commission noted: "In these states, candidates in 'safe' districts and not involved in competitive races usually opted for public financing to pay for their campaigns, because the expenditure limits were high enough and the money the program provided was sufficient to pay for such races. Yet, in races in competitive districts or in which a strong challenger sought to unseat an incumbent, the candidates did not accept public financing and consequently were not bound by an expenditure limit and . . . could spend as much money as they deemed necessary."[56]

## Innovation at the Local Level

Just as the push for state public funding of elections has gained momentum in the late 1980s, so has the drive to extend such programs to the local level. Prior to the mid-1980s, only Seattle featured such a scheme, and that program— first enacted in 1978—lapsed in 1982 due to a "sunset" provision. It was reenacted in 1984 and has served as a model for other municipal programs, including the one adopted by surrounding King County, Washington, in November 1989.

Tucson, Arizona, was the second municipality to enact public financing, leading several cities and counties that have taken the step over the past half-decade. Approved in November 1985 by a narrow 52 to 48 percent margin, Tucson's first publicly funded election occurred in 1987. It was considered a success; several candidates who rejected public funds said they would accept them the next time around, and others said that the accompanying spending limits had encouraged a more grass roots, less media-oriented, campaign on the part of the candidates.[57]

Two California municipalities followed suit. Sacramento County, California, was the third local government to approve public financing of elections, in an initiative in November 1986. The system was first implemented in June 1988, when few candidates were running. None of them actually received public funding.[58] That same year, the Sacramento program was thrown into question by the passage of statewide Proposition 73, which barred public funding of elections in California. The Sacramento system was challenged in the courts, where a lower court found for the primacy of the state prohibition;[59] this decision was not appealed by Sacramento County.

That judicial decision first seemed to doom a public financing ordinance approved by the voters of Los Angeles, the nation's second-largest city, in June 1990. Suit to stop public financing, based on the Sacramento County case, was brought, and while a lower court agreed with the decision, a court of appeals reversed it. The case is now being appealed to the state supreme court.[60] The original vote followed an ethics controversy involving the city's longtime mayor, Tom Bradley.

The country's most extensive local public financing program is located in the largest city, New York. As in Los Angeles across the country and New Jersey just across the Hudson River, New York City's program was born of scandal—the one that enveloped Mayor Edward Koch during his third term in office and led to formal charges of corruption against some of Koch's closest associates. Koch signed public financing legislation passed by the City Council in February 1988 and ran for reelection under its provisions a year later, losing to Manhattan borough president David N. Dinkins in the Democratic primary election.

Ironically, just as many states have been ahead of the federal government in experimenting with and implementing public funding of elections, both New York and Los Angeles have been ahead of the states in which they are located. Prior to the Proposition 73 vote barring public financing in California, the state legislature had twice passed public funding bills, only to see them vetoed by the governor. In New York, the city's adoption of public financing stands in stark contrast to the state legislature, which has been widely criticized from many quarters—including the state's Commission on Government Integrity—for failing to act on campaign finance reform.

Mayoral candidates participating in New York City's program had to limit contributions from any individual, corporation, union, or PAC to

$3,000 per election, and for other local offices the limits were even less; at the state level, the limit is a far more permissive $50,000. "Certainly the impact of large contributions was diminished considerably, and new patterns of fundraising became necessary," said Joseph A. O'Hare, chairman of the city's Campaign Finance Board, in assessing the 1989 elections. "A most encouraging sign of the program's impact is the substantial increase of the role played by small givers."[61]

The program appears to have worked better in the high-profile mayor's race —in which five of the six major candidates participated— and in boroughwide contests than in councilmanic races, where historically competition is low and machine politics has dominated.[62] Of the $4.5 million in public funds given to candidates, the qualifying mayoral candidates received a total of $2.8 million. Public funding represented slightly more than 12 percent of Dinkins's total expenditures in the primary and general election; Republican nominee Rudolph Giuliani financed almost a fifth of his campaign with public funds.[63] Circumstances changed, however, in 1991, when the number of seats was increased from thirty-five to fifty-one and there were many open seats and liberalized qualification requirements for eligibility to receive public funds. In the newly competitive City Council environment, participation in the program increased substantially, as did the public monies. Participation in the public funding system by contestants for City Council was not as high in 1991 as for other offices, except in special circumstances such as open seats.

## Public Funding and Public Opinion

It is evident that the success of public funding programs hinges on the amount of money provided to candidates and the degree to which they can supplant less desirable sources of campaign income. In turn, the availability of such funding to candidates depends on income tax checkoffs and legislative appropriations. In both instances, the issue comes down to one of support by the voting—and taxpaying—public.

In recent years, the news has not been particularly good. The public tends to be fickle when it comes to campaigns and elections, just as it is when the subject is budget deficits. Nobody likes a large deficit, but few want to close it by raising taxes or seeing a favored government program cut. Likewise, the public has a low opinion of the integrity of its elected servants but is ambivalent about using its tax dollars to supplant the largess of the wealthy magnate or well-heeled political action committee.

New Jersey taxpayers remain more supportive of public financing than their counterparts in other states. But even in New Jersey, there has been a decline in participation in the income tax checkoff from a high of 41.7 percent in 1980 to 32.3 percent in 1988. The drop in other states has been more precipitous. In Michigan, the rate has gone from 28.3 percent in 1977 to 14 percent in 1988, and there is concern that the program may lack adequate funding by the time of the 1994 gubernatorial contest. Minnesota and Wisconsin have experienced similar declines, as have states with a tax checkoff for political party funding. It is premature to say that public funding at the state level is in jeopardy. But recent experience has demonstrated problems that need to be addressed.

In June 1988, Rutgers' Eagleton Institute and the Newark *Star-Ledger* polled New Jersey voters on campaign finance and legislative elections. Three-quarters of those polled believed that too much money is being spent on state legislative contests and that spending and contribution limits should be imposed. A majority, however, did not favor public financing for legislative contests.[64]

California voters, polled in January 1990 in the wake of a major corruption investigation in their state capital, were asked about campaign finance. The results: Three-quarters of those responding advocated banning private contributions and providing tax dollars to pay for legislative races. And two-thirds even said they would "be willing to have a dollar or two added" to their state income tax to finance all political campaigns in the state.[65]

But ironically, California has a tax add-on in operation, which in recent years has brought in a paltry total of about $250,000 per tax year. And on Election Day 1990, when the voters had a chance to adopt public financing of legislative elections, they responded by defeating the initiative in question—Proposition 131—by an overwhelming margin.

# Chapter 3

# The Fifty-Headed Regulator

Several years ago, an enterprising member of Ohio's state capital press corps decided to take an in-depth look at the financing of legislative races in the state. As a first step, he set out to collect campaign reports filed by candidates for the Ohio Senate and House of Representatives. It was not long before he threw up his hands in frustration. The reason: Ohio makes no provision for state legislative campaign reports to be filed in a central location. Instead of taking a quick trip to the secretary of state's office in Columbus and photocopying collected filings, journalists—along with other members of the public seeking to monitor trends in Ohio campaign finance—must attempt to track down the reports at the multitude of county courthouses around the state. That, in turn, puts them at the mercy of the understaffed offices of county clerks, where coming to the aid of a disembodied voice on the other end of a long distance call from the state capital is rarely a priority. In some of Ohio's sixty-four counties, clerks' offices insist on photocopying fees of one dollar or more per page when a report is requested.[1] Indiana has a similar system, and a number of states charge up to $1.50 per page for photocopying.

Granted, not all states make it as difficult as Ohio or Indiana to obtain campaign finance reports; most do require candidates for state legislative as well as statewide office to file at a central location. But even among states that provide ready access to the information, it is the exception to find a state election agency that analyzes the volumes of reports it receives and publishes the data in a manner designed to enlighten the voting public.

"The Federal Election Commission keeps track of statistics on congressional races, but nobody has ever done a comprehensive survey on state legislative races (across the country)," Sandra Singer, then a staff member of the National Conference of State Legislatures, noted in a 1989 paper on the financing of such races. "The simple and rational reason for this is that it is currently impossible."[2]

The notion that office seekers should be forced to reveal who contributes to their increasingly expensive campaigns and how they spend the money enjoys widespread support; even those who reject more activist forms of campaign finance reform on ideological or pragmatic grounds tend to endorse the concept of disclosure. Thus, one would expect state governments to do a good job of distilling and publicizing the data that candidates file with them. But almost two decades after the Federal Election Campaign Act imposed comprehensive disclosure in presidential and congressional races, the states have not followed suit in many instances.

Sandra Singer comments, "Although almost all states have some type of filing requirements for campaign finance disclosure reports, very few states actually compile this data. Some review a small percentage of these reports randomly. Others simply place them in a file and forget them."[3] Adds Ruth Jones, "Fewer than half of the states publish a synthesis or summary of campaign finance data, and it is the rare agency . . . that ventures to provide position papers, analyses and policy recommendations or policy relevant summaries."[4]

A subsequent study by Common Cause of Ohio indicated that of forty-one states responding to a questionnaire, twenty-eight claimed to maintain some form of computerized system for compiling political fund data. But only fifteen publish reports on campaign finance.[5] Examination of the reports reveals wide variation in the kinds of data and the candidates or political committees covered.

Perhaps the point is best illustrated by the differences between the nation's two most populous states. California has one of the country's most comprehensive disclosure statutes. Its election commission publishes occasional analyses of the materials it receives, and the state issues extensive summaries containing detailed contribution listings.[6] On the other hand, New York issued no figures on campaign receipts or expenditures until prodded by its own Commission on Government Integrity. The State Board of Elections then published financial summaries of each Assembly and Senate campaign in 1988 but no contribution listings and no aggregate data.[7] Commendable comprehensive reports listing political finance data are issued by Alaska, Idaho, Missouri, New Jersey, Kentucky, and Washington, among others.

The inconsistent nature of disclosure in the fifty states, while an important issue in and of itself, points to even a larger problem: the continuing resistance to reform among many who sit in governors' mansions and state legislative chambers across the nation. To some extent, this resistance has been overt. In the mid-1980s, when momentum in favor of public financing of elections was building in states of varying size and philosophy, the governors of California and Illinois—the nation's first- and sixth-largest states—vetoed public funding bills. As will be detailed later, the California veto touched off years of political stalemate during which the public financing issue moved from the legislature to the voters by way of initiatives before ending up in the courts, which gutted the law.

But in many states, the roadblocks to reform have been more subtle. A law is passed in response to perceptions of scandal or to squelch a public outcry; it is only after the excitement dies down that it is discovered that self-interested legislators have inserted a clause here and a provision there to limit the statute's effectiveness.

In other instances, state legislatures have passed laws only to repeal them quietly when the attention span of the public has waned. In the case of Ohio, the legislature in 1974 enacted a measure with contribution and expenditure limits that then governor John Gilligan hailed as "one of the best" such laws in the country.[8] In 1976, the Supreme Court, in its *Buckley v. Valeo* decision, ruled expenditure limits to be an unconstitutional abridgment of the First Amendment, unless a candidate accepted them voluntarily in exchange for public financing. But in revising state law to comply with the *Buckley* decision, the Ohio legislature went a step further and also repealed the contribution limits, notwithstanding the Supreme Court's ruling that such restrictions were within the bounds of constitutionality.[9]

In yet other cases, the problem has not been the law itself but the implementation of it. When it comes to disclosure statutes, many states have adequate laws. In fact, forty-eight of fifty now call for both pre- and postelection reporting of contributions and expenditures.[10] The stumbling block is frequently money, sometimes the legislative appropriations process. The obstacles election commissions already face in compiling data have been aggravated in recent years by spending cuts in many states. This has prompted cutbacks among the few state agencies that have done meaningful analyses. It also has meant delays in the availability of the information and financial barriers to those interested in gathering it, often in the form of high photocopying charges.

"In state after state, agencies that prepare and publish official reports that now provide the best data sources for systematic analysis are under attack," Ruth Jones writes. "Thus, at the very time that more and more attention is being focused on the role of states, and more and more critical decisions are being made by elected state officials, we are likely to learn less and less about how the election campaigns of these state officials are financed."[11]

That is exactly the way some legislators like it. At a time when the public is concerned about the high cost of campaigns, not all incumbents are fully comfortable with seeing the sum total of their spending in bold headlines. And as the public grows more cynical about the influence of special interests in politics, state legislators are hardly eager to make data available that show more and more of their funds are coming from political action committees or wealthy individuals.

A recent study by the *Akron Beacon Journal* indicated why many of Ohio's legislators would prefer to make state capital reporters scurry around to sixty-four different courthouses in the state. A sampling of legislators' reports indicated that much of the money ostensibly collected for campaign expenses is quietly being transferred to pay for a variety of personal expenses.[12]

## State Election Agencies: Muzzling the Watchdog

In addition to serving as a clearinghouse for information, election commissions on both the federal and state levels have multiple roles as judge, jury, administrator, prosecutor, enforcer, and magistrate. The potential for conflict among these roles is clear. Strong enforcement of the law must not chill free speech or citizen participation. On the other hand, a weak enforcement policy does little to promote confidence in the electoral process. Unfortunately, legislators at both the federal and state levels have often ensured minimal effectiveness by the manner in which they have chosen to vest the responsibility for enforcement of election laws.

At the federal level, leading members of Congress resisted the concept of an independent election enforcement agency for almost a decade prior to agreeing to creation of the Federal Election Commission in 1974. In doing so, Congress sought to hold the new agency in check by reserving to itself the right to appoint four of six commission members. When this ploy was ruled unconstitutional by the Supreme Court as a violation of the separation of powers between the executive and legislative branches,[13] Congress responded by strictly limiting the circumstances under which the FEC could issue advisory opinions or conduct investigations or audits.

Similarly, a 1985 survey by Robert Huckshorn found that more than one-half of the states—twenty-six—had created special boards or commissions to administer campaign statutes. But only sixteen of these bodies had the power to levy fines. And of those sixteen, Huckshorn said that three-quarters of them were "limited either by restrictive statutory provisions or self-imposed limits that cast their application of civil penalties into the nuisance mold of traffic tickets."[14]

In the states that lack specially created agencies to oversee election laws, the responsibility generally has been placed with the secretary of state or comparable official. This official is typically either appointed by the governor or elected statewide. Ruth Jones warns, "Where [campaign finance] data are under the direct jurisdiction of an elected, partisan official, there is the potential for misuse, abuse or strategic obfuscation."[15]

In California, where responsibility is divided between the secretary of state and Fair Political Practices Commission, the FPPC imposed $20,000 in fines on Secretary of State March Fong Eu and supporters for filing required reports two years late. Embarrassed because her office receives the campaign fund reports, Secretary Eu said she was not aware her supporters had failed to file. However, the FPPC insisted she should have been aware and taken appropriate steps.[16]

Politics also frequently enters the equation in terms of enforcement. With the known exception of Nebraska, state election commissions have only civil prosecutorial authority and must refer criminal violations to the appropriate enforcement official. This is normally the state attorney general or local district attorney, who is a partisan official with legal discretion as to whether to pursue the matter. Few violations, however, can be classified as "knowing and willful"—the uniform standard across the country for criminal prosecution. In New Jersey, for example, there has been only one criminal prosecution for violation of the state's campaign disclosure law since its passage in 1973.[17]

At least a third of the state agencies responsible for regulating campaign finance do not have the authority to inititate inquiries into possible irregularities, and almost half lack the authority to subpoena witnesses and records.[18] Most state election agencies also lack auditors and investigators to carry out these functions, and many appear to rely largely on newspaper articles and public complaints rather than initiating actions on their own.

Frank Sorauf of the University of Minnesota writes, "If it is the case that the effectiveness of the FEC is hampered primarily by its relationships with Congress, it is even truer that state legislators have hesitated to create strong and effective agencies for regulating their own campaign finance."[19]

## The Best of the Bunch

While there is no empirical way to determine which states have the best systems for collecting campaign finance information and enforcing election laws, there are a handful of states often singled out for their efforts.

Election commissions in Connecticut, Florida, Minnesota, Washington, and Wisconsin are frequently mentioned; California's Fair Political Practices Commission and New Jersey's Election Law Enforcement Commission often top the list.

California's FPPC publishes campaign finance data by legislative district and political committee,[20] highlighting the percentage increases in aggregate contributions and disbursements from the election two years earlier. New Jersey's ELEC, in detailed studies of the state's gubernatorial elections, has examined not only where the money comes from but where it goes, with special emphasis on media costs.[21] Such studies are essential in determining why campaign costs are rising so much faster than inflation. ELEC also has published a series of white papers including "Trends in Legislative Campaign Financing: 1977–1987"[22] and an analysis leading to an endorsement of "Legislative Public Financing."[23] The Alaska Public Officers Commission has issued overviews of group, party, and PAC activity,[24] while the Washington Public Disclosure Commission has published analyses of political spending by major interest groups and other studies.[25] Any such publications can trigger criticism of the state agency, yet some manage to overcome the attacks and in the process disseminate meaningful information to the public.

While they share praise for their activities, the various commissions differ markedly in the manner in which they are funded. At present, the California FPPC is the only state election agency that is constitutionally guaranteed partial budgetary independence; additional funding has been supplied by the legislature.[26] New Jersey ELEC, on the other hand, stands as an example of the budgetary pressures that have buffeted similar agencies across the country, where the lack of real dollar increases in constant dollars prevents functions such as full computerization (see Table 1).

Ironically, as the New Jersey legislature in 1989 was sharply increasing the amount of public funding available to gubernatorial candidates, it reduced ELEC's administrative budget by more than 12 percent.[27] The action came in the face of a dramatic increase in requests from the public for information as compared with the previous year.[28]

The major impact of the cuts has been on the commission's enforcement functions. The ELEC subdivisions responsible for reviewing campaign disclosure reports and investigating and prosecuting civil violations have fewer staff members than at any time in the past decade. In 1989, ELEC brought 542 civil complaints and conducted 104 investigations; in 1990, the commission expected to bring about two-thirds fewer complaints and conduct only half that number of investigations.[29]

**Table 1**
Increasing Responsibility, Decreasing Resources:
The Fiscal Crunch Faced by a Leading State Election Commission

New Jersey Election Law Enforcement Commission
Legislative Appropriations, Fiscal Years 1986–1991

| Year | Amount[a] | Percent Increase/ Decrease | Staff Members | Percent Increase/ Decrease |
|---|---|---|---|---|
| 1986 | $ 912,000 | +17.5 | 28 | unchanged |
| 1987 | 1,059,000 | +16 | 30 | +7 |
| 1988 | 1,127,000 | +6.5 | 32 | +6.5 |
| 1989 | 1,235,000 | +9.5 | 32 | unchanged |
| 1990 | 1,208,000 | -2 | 34 | +6 |
| 1991 | 1,062,000 | -12 | 28 | -18 |

Source: New Jersey Election Law Enforcement Commission.
[a]The above amounts do not include public funds made available to New Jersey gubernatorial candidates.

In response to the problem, ELEC has suggested a number of ways to raise additional funds, including imposing fees on those that generate the agency's workload: PACs, lobbyists, and political parties. ELEC is now allowed to retain the fines it collects, which totaled about $40,000 in 1989. It is looking into whether to stiffen such fines by imposing them on each transaction that violates the state's disclosure law; at present, the fines are imposed on a per report basis. "It may be time to review seriously how ethics agencies in New Jersey and across the nation fit into the structure of government," Frederick M. Herrmann, ELEC's veteran executive director, wrote recently. He asked rhetorically: "Should an ethics agency that regulates the campaigns of officeholders be dependent on them for its funding?"[30]

In earlier years, enforcement across the country was light because the commissions' purpose was to educate the candidates and committee operatives about the requirements of new laws. Now some laws have been in effect fifteen years or more, and some commissions are determined to impose fines for every significant infraction. California's Fair Political Practices Commission has a policy to fine each violation $2,000; whereas earlier a candidate or political action or party committee found to have committed five violations might have bargained for a lesser combined fine, now it is certain to receive a $10,000 bill. The Florida agency's assessments are now dedicated to a public financing program—

as will be discussed later—that has suffered due to the legislature's unwillingness to provide additional sources of funding.

## Disclosure: Plugging the Holes

While all states have disclosure laws on the books, there are wide variations in their stringency as well as in the vigor with which they are enforced.

Federal law requires that any committee that raises or spends more than $1,000 register with the Federal Election Commission and designate a treasurer. But at the state level, certain types of political committees often are exempt from filing. New Jersey—frequently cited as the home of one of the country's model campaign finance laws—does require candidates to report PAC contributions, but does not require the PACs themselves to register with the Election Law Enforcement Commission. "Consequently, the public does not have a clear sense of which interests they represent," says Herrmann.[31]

The New Jersey disclosure statute reflects another failing of many state laws in that they frequently require only limited information about a candidate's contributors. In its recent recommendations for improving New Jersey campaign finance laws, the Ad Hoc Commission on Legislative Ethics and Campaign Finance stated: "The commission believes that more information must be required from individuals and organizations which make campaign contributions and that information must be readily available to the public. . . . The public does not now know whether a person contributes to a candidate because he simply agrees with the candidate's stand on certain issues or because he is seeking to promote a particular issue favored by the members of his occupation or his employer."[32]

A similar problem exists in states that permit so-called conduit or pipeline contributions (Ohio is a notable example). As noted in Chapter 1, this device is frequently used by powerful legislators to fill their campaign coffers while getting around the state's prohibition on corporate donations.[33] As a result, it becomes virtually impossible for the public to tell how much money a legislator is getting from powerful lobbying interests.

The provision for conduit contributions, quietly inserted when the Ohio legislature passed a sweeping campaign reform measure in 1974, allows employees to donate money through payroll deductions. Theoretically, these employees designate which candidate will receive their money. In practice, the employees tend to follow the guidance of their employer or, in some cases, grant their supervisor power of attorney to make such a designation.

These contributions are then "bundled" and given to a candidate on a corporate check, so that the recipient is made aware of his or her bene-factor. The catch is that, when the donations are disclosed, candidates do not have to make any reference to the company writing the check. Rather, the money coming in shows up on disclosure reports as numer-ous small contributions from individuals.

"Thanks to this huge loophole, a cottage industry of political consultants thrives in Columbus, showing corporations how to beat disclosure requirements," the Cleveland *Plain Dealer* declared in an editorial.[34]

To demonstrate the difficulty of tracing the source of these conduit contributions, consider the effort undertaken by three reporters for the *Akron Beacon Journal* in examining donations to committees associated with two of Ohio's most powerful politicians: Democratic House speaker Vernal G. Riffe, Jr., and Republican Senate president Stanley J. Aronoff.

First, the journalists entered into a personal computer the names of all contributors to committees controlled by Riffe and Aronoff between 1986 and 1988. After creating a list of more than 15,300 individuals, the reporters used the addresses listed to break down the names by coun-ty and city of residence. Using city directories, they then sought to identify as many donors as possible by occupation and employer. It soon became apparent that utility company employees were showing up in disproportionately large numbers. They then obtained company direc-tories and public documents listing utility company employees. Ultimately, the reporters identified the individuals responsible for some $2.4 million, or about three-quarters of the money given to Riffe and Aronoff during this period. It took six months to complete this enter-prising newspaper investigation.[35]

In late 1989, Common Cause filed complaints with the secretary of state's office and the Ohio Elections Commission seeking an investigation of this "hidden pipeline of giving." The Elections Commission held a hearing and voted to dismiss the complaint, saying that it was outside the agency's jurisdiction.[36] Secretary of State Sherrod Brown then agreed to investigate, but his defeat in the November 1990 election placed the future of the matter in doubt.

The increasing use of so-called independent expenditure campaigns at the state level also is certain to test the adequacy of many state dis-closure laws. Numerous states already have statutes that address inde-pendent spending by requiring reports from all individuals and groups that raise or spend money related to political campaigns. But, once again, the detail and timeliness of these reports vary widely from state to state.[37]

# Sidetracking Public Financing: Florida, Maryland, and Rhode Island

The combination of tight budgets and legislative recalcitrance has not only hindered implementation of such basic elements of campaign regulation as disclosure and enforcement. In two states, it has served for a time to derail ambitious plans for public financing of state elections. In a third state, public financing was approved by the legislature only to be undercut by political maneuvering among the candidates themselves.

In Florida, now the nation's fourth-largest state, the legislature in 1986 approved a program of partial public financing for the statewide contests, including the governorship and six cabinet offices. Because the state lacks an income tax, the program was to be funded through state appropriations as well as fines paid by election law violators.[38]

State political observers say that the driving force behind passage of the measure was the then speaker of the Florida House, Democrat James Harold Thompson. However, under Florida's legislative system, the speaker must step down after serving only one term. Thompson left office at the end of 1986 and his successor, Democrat Jon Mills, was far less sympathetic to the concept of public financing. In addition, Florida in 1986 elected a Republican governor, Bob Martinez, who was opposed on pragmatic as well as ideological grounds. Martinez was facing a tough reelection fight in 1990, and had no desire to provide public subsidies to help a Democratic opponent gain statewide name recognition.

The upshot was that a plan to have $12 million in the state campaign fund by 1990 never materialized. When the law was first enacted, the legislature set aside $3 million as a first installment. But a fiscal crunch caused the legislature to rescind the appropriation just months after it had been approved. No further funds were appropriated for the 1990 elections, largely because of the presence of a hostile governor and legislative leadership.

Without legislative appropriations, the state's election trust fund was left with a very limited amount of money from election-related fines. In 1988, special elections were held for two statewide offices, secretary of state and insurance commissioner. One candidate running for insurance commissioner received $47,707 in subsidies and another seeking the secretary of state's position received $49,681. In return, they agreed to spending limits in the area of $820,000.[39] Both were beaten, however, by candidates who refused public financing and heavily outspent them.

In 1990, only one candidate—a Republican running for state agriculture commissioner—sought and qualified for public financing. He received approximately $75,000, leaving the state trust fund with about $275,000 as of late 1990. Neither Martinez nor his Democratic opponent, ex-senator Lawton Chiles, sought public funding in the gubernatorial race. Had they opted to do so, they would have been compelled to limit their spending to 75 cents for each vote cast in the 1986 governor's contest. That comes to almost $2.54 million each. Unfettered by spending limits, Martinez spent about $10.6 million and Chiles $5.4 million.

Ironically, Martinez, who had feared that public funding would aid a lesser-known opponent, ended up losing the governorship to a man with almost universal name recognition. Governor-elect Chiles—who refused to take contributions in excess of $100 during his campaign—then promoted a new system of state support for the public financing program of statewide races—one with ensured funding; funds are transferred from the state's General Revenue Fund to the Election Campaign Financing Trust Fund without an appropriation. This, along with contribution limits of $500 per election, was enacted within four months of Chiles taking office.

In Maryland, a public financing program has been on the books since 1974. But it has yet to be put into operation.[40] As with a number of other public funding programs, Maryland's was born of concern with both real and perceived corruption. Like New Jersey, which enacted its program the same year, Maryland had long been regarded as one of the most corrupt states in the nation. That image was reinforced in late 1973, when Vice President Spiro Agnew pleaded no contest to a single charge of tax evasion and resigned from office. Agnew's action was part of a plea bargain arising from allegations that he had taken kickbacks on public contracts while serving as Baltimore County executive and governor of Maryland during the mid-1960s.

When the legislature responded the next year by approving a plan calling for partial public funding for primaries and full funding for general elections, opponents managed to attach what was regarded as a "killer amendment." On the surface, the amendment had a noble purpose: rather than limiting public funding to statewide races, it would extend to state legislative campaigns as well. But proponents of public funding charged that the amendment was designed to undermine the program by spreading the money too thin.

That is exactly what happened. An "add-on" option on Maryland income tax forms allowing taxpayers to contribute $2 above and beyond their tax liability failed to yield nearly enough money to fund the program. This caused public funding, originally scheduled to take effect in 1978, to be postponed that year and again in 1982. In 1984, the legislature, deciding the plan was never going to work, voted to do away with the

$2 add-on. But the money already in the fund continued to collect interest; by 1990, it totaled about $2.3 million.

There have been several attempts to divert the "Fair Campaign Financing Fund" for other purposes. However, the state's then attorney general, Stephen Sachs, said in a 1981 opinion that the legislature lacked the authority to do so because the money represented voluntary contributions collected for a specific purpose. "The state, as trustee, thus has a duty to use the fund in accordance with the general purpose of the trust," Sachs declared in ruling that the state had a contractual obligation to the donors.[41]

Nevertheless, in 1989, Governor William Donald Schaefer (who had beaten Sachs for the Democratic gubernatorial nomination in 1986) proposed that the trust fund be used for voter registration and education. Common Cause of Maryland threatened to sue to ensure that the money be retained for candidate support, and the legislature backed off.[42] Like his Republican counterpart in Florida, Schaefer had little desire to provide a Republican challenger with public funds when he sought reelection in 1990.[43] Under a bill passed just before Schaefer took office, the funds had been scheduled for use during the 1990 campaign. While declining to use the money for voter registration and education as Schaefer wanted, the legislature in 1989 did enact a measure that postponed use of the money remaining in the trust fund until 1994—when Schaefer would be forced by law to retire after serving two terms.

As matters now stand, the trust fund will be allocated to gubernatorial candidates two decades after it was first created, and if that occurs, it will be the end of public financing in Maryland. With the scandals surrounding Agnew and his Democratic successor, Marvin Mandel, now a distant memory, advocates of public funding see little pressure from the voting public for such a program.

"We don't hear any clamor or obvious support," says Phil Andrews, executive director of Common Cause in Maryland. If the tax add-on was revived, he added, "it would take a good amount of education for the public to contribute to it in significant numbers."[44]

In Rhode Island, the state legislature was left with no choice but to enact public funding for gubernatorial campaigns following a 1986 voter referendum on the issue. In passing the program, the legislature included a provision requiring use of appropriations to make up the difference between public subsidies given to candidates and the amount raised through an income tax checkoff.

Notwithstanding approval by both the voters and the legislature, Rhode Island's public funding program failed its first test in the 1990 gubernatorial elections. One candidate flatly refused to participate, and two others used that as a reason not to accept public funding and abide by the accompanying spending limits. As a result, only one of the aspirants in the Democratic primary opted for public funding, and neither candidate in the general election ended up doing so.

The problems began in late 1989, when word began to filter out that two leading candidates—Governor Edward DiPrete, a Republican, and Providence mayor Joseph Paolino, a Democrat—might use the state's worsening financial condition as a pretext not to accept public funding. This, in turn, would free the two candidates—both of whom had raised large amounts of money—from the need to abide by the legislated spending limit ($1.5 million if a candidate did not face a primary, $2 million if he or she did).

In early 1990, Common Cause of Rhode Island sought to gain commitments from all potential candidates to participate in the public funding program. Two Democrats, former lieutenant governor Richard Licht (who was to drop out of the race prior to the primary) and Warwick mayor Francis Flaherty, said that they would. A third Democrat, millionaire businessman Bruce Sundlun, said that he would if the other candidates did. Paolino sidestepped the question, citing the fact that he was not yet a formal candidate. And DiPrete said that his participation would depend on several circumstances, including the condition of the state budget.[45]

A month later, Common Cause again wrote to the candidates, offering to mediate the issue. What followed was a series of meetings involving representatives of DiPrete and the three Democrats remaining in the race: Flaherty, Sundlun, and Paolino. DiPrete complained that because he faced no primary opposition, he was restricted to $500,000 less in overall spending despite constant attacks from his three potential Democratic opponents. Ultimately, DiPrete, Flaherty, and Sundlun agreed to a scheme whereby the $500,000 difference could be made up from DiPrete's share of the proceeds of a party fund-raising dinner attended by President Bush in late 1989.[46] But Paolino declined to go along, and the agreement collapsed. Only Flaherty, lagging behind the other candidates in fund-raising, agreed to stay within the limits and accept public funding.

The upshot was a $10.4 million gubernatorial race in the smallest state by area. The eventual winner, Sundlun, spent $4.1 million to get through the primary and general election—twice what he would have been allowed if he had participated in the public funding program. Of this, $3.4 million came from loans made by Sundlun to his own campaign.[47]

Legislation subsequently introduced in the 1991 session of the Rhode Island legislature sought to limit a candidate's contributions to his or her own campaign to no more than 5 percent of total expenditures. In a reference to newly elected Governor Sundlun, it was dubbed the "anti-Bruce bill." It did not pass in the 1991 session.

Paolino ran a poor third in the September primary. With total expenditures of $3.2 million, his campaign ended up spending a hefty $69.45 for each of the 46,074 votes he gained. Reform advocates, noting that Paolino and Sundlun were even in the polls as of early summer, contend that a blitz of Paolino television ads and mailings prior to the primary backfired.

"I think people were fed up," remarked Phil West, whose organization, Common Cause, publicly blamed Paolino for the failure of efforts to put a lid on spending in the 1990 race. "While most people didn't know exactly how much was being spent [by Paolino], they thought it was too much."[48]

## Taking the Initiative: Public Demand for Reform

While resistance to election reform persists in many state legislatures, the public has increasingly taken matters into its own hands. During the past two decades, there have been some twenty-two instances in which issues relating to the financial conduct of campaigns ended up on state or local ballots and eighteen of them passed—a remarkable outcome (see Appendix 3). In three states—Hawaii, Minnesota, and Rhode Island—public financing of elections has been enacted or expanded by popular vote. And citizens in several municipalities, including New York City and Los Angeles, have approved public funding by means of referenda or initiatives.

A stagnant legislative process invites election reform by initiative. But the use of the initiative to impose campaign reform has proved no less controversial than those instances when it has been used to reduce auto insurance rates, cut taxes, or stiffen environmental laws. In California, where the initiative has become an integral part of the political culture, attempts to bring about public funding of elections by popular vote have yielded controversy, confusion, and judicial intervention in place of reform.

Obviously, the initiative process provides a means by which the public can bypass a governor and legislature more interested in political self-preservation than changes in the rules of the electoral game. At times, it can be used to prod a legislative body into action; in 1973–74, the Massachusetts legislature voted to establish a system of campaign disclosure and an independent election agency in the face of an effort to put a similar proposal on the ballot. Finally, in the case of public funding of elections, use of the initiative involves rank-and-file citizens at the ground floor of the superstructure of politics. This, in turn, may help to encourage voters to continue to support the system as taxpayers in the years to come.

On the downside, initiatives placed before the voters— be they related to campaign reform or other issues—frequently represent the views of a single group of individuals or an organization, as opposed to the consensus and compromise that result from the legislative process. The legislative system provides the opportunity for fact-finding and fine-tuning in committee hearings and floor debate, and offers greater likelihood that the final product will function effectively as well as stand up before any legal and constitutional challenges. While some reformers may believe that a campaign reform measure ratified by the voters is less vulnerable to being struck down in court than a law crafted by the legislature, the California experience suggests that this is not the case.

### California: Rival Propositions Produce "Legal Nightmare"

In 1984, the California legislature passed a campaign reform bill, only to see it vetoed by Republican governor George Deukmejian because it provided for public funding. That same year, a group of prominent Californians—including many business executives—formed the private California Commission on Campaign Financing. In publishing its comprehensive study of California campaign finance in 1985, the group drafted a model law pertaining to races for the state Senate and Assembly, including public funding provisions. After failing to make headway in the legislature, California Common Cause and others turned the proposal to the ballot box.[49]

But when proponents submitted signatures necessary to get the measure on the ballot, the California secretary of state ruled that there were an insufficient number for the proposal to be put on the November 1986 ballot. In response, Common Cause, the major backer of the effort, took the unprecedented step of scrutinizing the signatures. After a lengthy process, Common Cause was successful in documenting that the measure had gained one hundred more valid signatures than necessary. At that point, the proposal was designated Proposition 68 and placed on the June 1988 primary ballot.

In response to Proposition 68, three maverick state legislators—a Republican, a Democrat, and an independent—drafted a rival initiative that made it onto the ballot as Proposition 73. Proposition 73 contained an outright ban on any form of public funding in the state of

California. It also sought to impose a detailed schedule of contribution limits and to apply them to all state races.

The business community, tired of being inundated with requests for donations, split over which measure to support. The state Chamber of Commerce switched its support from Proposition 68 to Proposition 73. The California Roundtable, another major business group, stayed with Proposition 68.

Then there was a third force: the no-no campaign. Its supporters included Assembly Speaker Willie Brown and Senate President Pro Tem David Roberti. Their concern: both Proposition 68 and Proposition 73 contained a ban on fund transfers between candidates, a device used heavily by Brown and Roberti to help favored candidates and secure their power bases in Sacramento.

Behind the no-no campaign were political consultants Michael Berman and Carl D'Agostino. Their firm, BAD Campaigns, was the strategic arm of the "Waxman–Berman" machine headed by U.S. representatives Henry Waxman and Howard Berman— Michael Berman's brother. This West Los Angeles organization owed much of its clout to the money it raised and directed to other candidates. Consequently, Michael Berman and D'Agostino produced highly controversial ads implying that the Ku Klux Klan and the Nazi party could benefit from public funding under Proposition 68.

Inevitably, the voting public was confused by the proliferation of choices and the conflicting claims. The no-no campaign spent most of its $1.3 million in an effort to defeat Proposition 68, whose backers spent about $800,000. Virtually ignored was Proposition 73, which had a shoestring budget of $30,000. On June 7, 1988, Proposition 68—which provided for public funding—won with 53 percent of the vote. But, to the surprise of the state's political establishment, Proposition 73—which barred public funding—also was approved. It gained 58 percent and thereby superseded Proposition 68.

"We won and we lost," lamented Walter Zelman, then executive director of Common Cause of California and a leading supporter of Proposition 68. "The voters, in their rush to support campaign finance reform, figured it would be a good idea to support both measures. But, by doing so, they diluted our effort. . . ."[50]

As it turned out, the fight was far from over. "We have a legal nightmare," California election attorney Lance Olson proclaimed following the vote.[51] The state's Fair Political Practices Commission found itself trying to interpret the will of the people, as reformers contended that about thirty provisions of Proposition 68 should be enforced on the grounds that they did not conflict with Proposition 73. The state Democratic party joined two major labor groups, the Service Employees International Union and the California Teachers Association, in challenging the constitutionality of Proposition 73.

On September 25, 1990, more than two years after voters had gone to the polls, U.S. District Judge Lawrence Karlton ruled that two key elements of Proposition 73—a $1,000 fiscal-year limit on individual campaign contributions and either a $2,500 or a $5,000 per year cap on donations from political committees—were unconstitutional. "I conclude that Proposition 73, in measuring the limitation on campaign contributions by fiscal year rather than election, unconstitutionally restricts free speech and favors incumbents against challengers," Karlton wrote in his decision, noting that challengers often do not decide to run until the year of an election.[52] Therefore, incumbents would gain a one-year head start in fund-raising. And, in a victory for political leaders such as Brown and Roberti, Karlton threw out the ban on transfers from one candidate to another, ruling that it violated First Amendment rights of free speech.

From a legal standpoint, the only major provisions of Proposition 73 left standing were the prohibition on public funding and restrictions on certain types of mass mailings by incumbent officeholders. Left untouched were the election agency, the Fair Political Practices Commission, and disclosure provisions of the Political Reform Act of 1974. From a political standpoint, Karlton's decision —coming in the home stretch of a campaign in which the governorship and six other statewide offices were up for grabs—had major ramifications.

"Once again, [the ruling] means we throw thousands and thousands of dollars at lawyers to tell us what to do," complained David Townsend, one of the state's leading political consultants.[53] An attempt to gain a stay of the decision brought one relating to legislative campaigns but not to statewide campaigns.[54]

The scramble for dollars that ensued in the wake of Karlton's ruling had less to do with philosophy or political affiliation than it did with the size of one's campaign treasury. Senator Pete Wilson, the Republican gubernatorial candidate, had a large lead in fund-raising over Democratic opponent Dianne Feinstein, the former mayor of San Francisco, at the time of Karlton's decision. Unsurprisingly, Wilson called on Feinstein to continue to comply voluntarily with Proposition 73's contribution limits. Equally unsurprisingly, Feinstein declined to accept Wilson's challenge. More than three-quarters of a million dollars poured into her campaign in the week following the ruling, primarily in the form of large gifts from labor unions, Hollywood supporters, and individuals associated with Feinstein's husband, a wealthy investment banker.[55]

While Wilson was challenging Feinstein to abide by the old limits, several of his Republican ticket mates did not hesitate to take advantage of the free-for-all, including GOP secretary of state candidate Joan Milke Flores. "It is the difference between winning and losing," Flores's chief fund-raiser, Joyce Valdez, said of her candidate's ability to raise large sums.[56]

As it turned out, Karlton's ruling was not the courts' last word before Election Day. On November 1, the California supreme court invalidated all provisions of Proposition 68. In doing so, it overturned a state court of appeals ruling a year earlier that said that several provisions of Proposition 68 not in conflict with Proposition 73 could take effect. The reasoning of the supreme court was that when two initiatives were presented as "all or nothing" alternatives or established a comprehensive regulatory scheme on the same subject, only the measure winning the most votes could be enforced. Otherwise, picking and choosing would create a regulatory plan not contemplated by the voters.[57]

The supreme court's action, coupled with Karlton's decision, left the state with only provisional limits on contributions to legislative candidates, notwithstanding the voters' choosing in June 1988 to adopt two initiatives containing more extensive ceilings. Reformers pinned their hopes on a new initiative, Proposition 131, which combined term limits on officeholders with public funding, expenditure ceilings, and contribution limits. But on November 6, 1990, voters rejected that proposition by an overwhelming 62–38 percent margin.

It was left to Attorney General John Van de Kamp, a leading backer of Proposition 131, to write a political epitaph. The court decision invalidating the contribution limits, he declared, "returns California politics to the law of the jungle."[58] Actually, he overstated his case somewhat, since prior to the two initiatives in 1988, California had no contribution limits whatsoever.

Two postscripts illustrate the continuing judicial involvement in California election law. First, appeals of Judge Karlton's decision and partial stay all the way to the U.S. Supreme Court brought no upset, but the federal court of appeals will review the ruling.[59] Second, a remaining portion of Proposition 73, prohibiting public funding in the state, has put the public financing programs of Los Angeles and Sacramento County in doubt; further appeals will be heard in these cases.[60]

## The Limits of Legislative Reform

As in the example of California, it is frequently those holding elective office who are the roadblocks to reform. But there are also instances when those in power do vote to bring about change, only to be stymied by the courts.

In 1989, the Florida legislature passed a law banning campaign contributions during the legislative session. The prohibition was aimed at the much-used "capital fund-raiser," a device used by members of the U.S. Congress as well as state legislators to collect money from lobbyists who feel they can ill afford not to give with major issues pending.

But in an action brought by a Republican candidate for state agriculture commissioner, a Florida trial court threw out the law as unconstitutional in early 1990, and the decision was later upheld by the Florida supreme court. The decision may affect nine other states where contributions from registered lobbyists are banned during the legislative session.

The Florida supreme court contended that the law represented an "overbroad intrusion upon the rights of free speech and associations." The court added, "In its commendable effort to stop the appearance of corruption caused by well-heeled special interests, the [law] imposes too heavy a hand on the innocent."[61] A similar result, it suggested, could be achieved through less restrictive means such as curtailing contributions from entities "found to be most involved in creating the appearance of corruption."[62]

In another 1990 case, the Wisconsin supreme court upheld a 1974 state law limiting the total amount of PAC money that a candidate may accept—so-called aggregate limits. The matter was appealed to the U.S. Supreme Court, which declined in early 1991 to review the case. However, with proposals to curtail the participation of PACs proliferating at the federal and state levels, it appears inevitable that the courts will be drawn increasingly into this issue. (See Chapter 4 for further discussion of the issues raised by the Wisconsin case.)

At issue was a ruling by the Wisconsin Elections Board in which a Republican assemblyman, John Gard, was found to have violated a rule that prevents candidates from accepting contributions from political action committees totaling more than 65 percent of the spending limit for that office. The U.S. Supreme Court's landmark *Buckley v. Valeo* decision held that spending limits may not be mandatory; they must be voluntarily accepted by candidates in return for such enticements as public funding. In part, Gard has argued that—even though he did not accept public funding—he is being forced to abide by an aggregate contribution limit that he considers to be a de facto spending limit.

Minnesota and New Hampshire are perhaps the two legislatures that have been most willing to explore the territory on which Congress has been reluctant to tread. Both may end up in court for doing so.

In 1989, New Hampshire enacted a law that waives a $5,000 filing fee as well as petition signature requirements for congressional candidates who agree to abide by spending limits. In late 1989, the Federal Election

Commission ruled that one provision of the law—an indirect restriction on the ability of state parties to spend money in federal elections—was preempted by federal statutes. So far, however, no one has come forward to challenge the balance of the law.[63]

In the next election, congressional candidates in New Hampshire appeared to be less concerned with constitutional questions than with the concern of voters over rising campaign costs. During the 1990 campaign, five Senate candidates and eleven House candidates said they would abide by the state spending limits,[64] which are $200,000 in House races and $400,000 in Senate races.

But New Hampshire legislators seem ready to go a step further. During their 1990 session, they came close to passing a limit on independent expenditure campaigns by PACs in congressional races. Passage of such legislation would be all but certain to invite a court challenge from one of the ever-growing number of federal PACs; the *Buckley v. Valeo* decision threw out restrictions on independent expenditure campaigns as unconstitutional.

A practical experience with the New Hampshire spending limit is revealing. In 1990, a U.S. Senate candidate, Democrat John Durkin, agreed to the $400,000 expenditure limit in his general election campaign. His Republican opponent, Robert Smith, spent more than $1 million, and, in addition, two groups undertook last-minute independent expenditures totaling at least $508,160 on his behalf. Smith won with 67 percent of the vote. Durkin had cast himself as a financial underdog by accepting the limits and also refusing to accept PAC contributions; but the independent expenditure campaign was unexpected and left Durkin without recourse late in the campaign.[65] This demonstrates a risk that candidates voluntarily limiting spending may face when court-protected, unlimited independent expenditures are thrown against them on behalf of their opponents.

In Minnesota, the 1990 legislature took the boldest step yet: it expanded the state's program of public financing for statewide and state legislative candidates to include congressional aspirants. The new law imposes spending limits of $3.4 milllion on U.S. Senate candidates and $425,000 on House candidates, and provides public funding equal to 25 percent of those spending limits.

The response from Washington, D.C., was both swift and predictable. "It is an unconstitutional bill that is preempted by federal law," said Benjamin L. Ginsberg, chief counsel for the Republican National Committee, which has long opposed spending limits and public financing of elections. "We will definitely challenge it."[66]

Although the outcome of the New Hampshire and Minnesota legislative efforts is not yet certain, preemption and federal supremacy likely will apply both to attempts to extend state law to cover congressional candidates from those states and to overcome U.S. Supreme Court doctrine on issues such as independent expenditures.[67] There are other potential points of collision between the state legislatures and the courts. Minnesota and Wisconsin, for example, provide public financing only for general election candidates but also limit expenditures in primary campaigns. No legal challenges have been made, even though the Supreme Court predicated expenditure limitations on the provision of public funds.

# Chapter 4

# Reforming the Reforms

By now, it is apparent that—despite the best of intentions—many of the campaign finance reforms adopted at the state level during the 1970s and 1980s fell short of the mark. In some cases, these laws simply took an existing problem and shifted it sideways. In other instances, the reforms actually created new and unforeseen problems.

This is not to disparage the accomplishments of the past two decades. All states now require disclosure of the amounts and sources of contributions, as well as data on disbursements, by candidates or political committees, or both. More than half of the states have limits on individual contributions, thus curtailing the role of the old-style political "fat cat." Perhaps most significantly, almost half the states have moved to provide political parties or candidates with some public subsidies or tax-assisted political financing, thereby lessening the dependence on private funds with real or perceived strings attached.

But a perusal of the political science literature of the mid-1970s reveals that the concerns that prompted the state-level reforms of that era were much the same as those of today. Campaign costs continue to escalate. Incumbent officeholders are less and less assailable by challengers. Where large contributors have been restricted, interest groups have rushed in to fill the void; their donations hardly seem more desirable than those of wealthy individuals. And half the states have yet to put any limits on PACs, a major source of controversial money.

The persistence and even intensification of campaign-related problems have spurred a widespread search for solutions. Over the past five years, the private California Commission on Campaign Financing has documented the ills plaguing the campaign finance system at the state and local levels and has recommended ways to mitigate them. In New York, Governor Mario Cuomo appointed a blue-ribbon commission that proposed a comprehensive reform package to a reluctant legislature. In New Jersey, with concern increasing about special interest money in legislative elections, an ad hoc commission put forth a lengthy list of recommendations. And other states have set up study groups to address the subject of money and politics.

As the states search for answers, the diversity of fifty political cultures will come to be important. What works in one state may not work in another. When the Council of Governmental Ethics Laws (COGEL) recently unveiled a model state law for campaign finance as well as government ethics, Raymond E. Wallace, executive director of the Kentucky Registry of Election Finance, observed, "It's a working document. I don't think states will ever run in tandem on something like this. To take it to a legislature and ask that they enact it in its entirety is pure folly."[1]

For example, an effort by New Hampshire to limit spending has had a mixed record of success, to say nothing of its questionable constitutionality. Yet in a relatively rural state with a tradition of fiscal tightfistedness and one-on-one campaigning, few candidates appeared willing to risk the wrath of the voters by refusing to go along. If such a provision were enacted in an a urban state with a population long accustomed to big-spending, television-oriented campaigns, it is a good bet that some office seeker would be in court in a matter of days. New Hampshire's tight-fistedness, incidentally, extends to seeking to get expenditure limitations on the cheap—using the low-cost lure of waived filing fees to gain compliance rather than appropriating money for public financing.

There are, however, several basic truths regarding the interaction of money and politics. These should be kept in mind in weighing a program of reform, regardless of a state's demographics, culture, or traditions.

## It Costs Money to Run Campaigns

Nostalgia buffs may long for the days when candidates kissed babies, marched in torchlight parades, and passed out sponges with their name that expanded when dunked in water. Those days are gone, and there is no way to bring them back. Even candidates for state legislature and city council now hire pollsters, direct mail consultants, and fundraisers. These services cost. The issue is not how to de-professionalize politics. Rather, it is how to pay for modern campaigns in a manner that reduces the opportunity for corruption or the appearance of corruption while instilling public confidence.

## Too Little Money Can Be as Harmful as Too Much

If high campaign costs can keep potential entrants out of the political arena, so can excessive limits on campaign money. Even taking away their ready access to political dollars, incumbents at the state and local as well as the federal level enjoy tremendous advantages due to widespread name recognition and the increasing perquisites of office. Legislators often are unwilling to eliminate the perks of office, which they see as representational necessities. For a challenger to overcome these requires an ample supply of cash—sufficient to get the name recognition necessary to contest an election effectively. If we are a generation away from emery boards and pencils emblazoned with a candidate's name, we are about 150 years past the time when an aspiring candidate could simply purchase a printing press and start his own newspaper as a platform. Today's means of political promotion, particularly television and radio advertising, are tremendously expensive. The 1976 Supreme Court ruling that mandatory spending limits in political campaigns are unconstitutional was a recognition that money cannot be neatly divorced from the First Amendment rights of free speech and free association.[2]

## Campaign Reform Often Meets the Law of Unforeseen Consequences

In 1979, amid complaints from state and local parties that public financing of presidential elections had cut them out of the process, Congress agreed to the seemingly modest step of allowing state and local party organizations to underwrite voter registration and get-out-the-vote drives benefiting presidential candidates. What resulted was the controversial "soft money" provision that allowed the parties to spend on behalf of Michael Dukakis and George Bush half as much again as the legislated spending limit during their 1988 campaigns. There are now widespread calls in Congress to undo what was done more than a decade ago.

The lesson here is that, given the pluralistic and dynamic nature of the American political system, campaign finance reform often does not work in the manner intended by its sponsors. That is not to deny that efforts should be made to improve the status quo; it simply means there are no panaceas or permanent solutions. As savvy political operatives and election lawyers find ways to get around existing laws in order to tap new sources of political money, the efficacy of these laws must constantly be reevaluated by their proponents.

## Campaign Money Does Not Exist in a Vacuum

Strict regulation of the ways a candidate raises and spends money on the campaign trail will come to little avail if that candidate confronts an "anything goes" atmosphere once he or she arrives at the state capital. According to Ruth Jones,

The laws changing how campaign money is raised and spent must be viewed in tandem with other reforms. These reforms include

1. public disclosure of decision-makers' finances and special interests,

2. open and above board policy making "in the sunshine,"

3. purging conflicts of interests, and

4. providing for a pluralist system of representation that works for all interests, not just those with special ties to the elected, or those who have resources to hire advocates to influence public policy outside the normal channels of public decision-making.[3]

Of course, plural representation turns on the presence of an involved electorate. The best of regulatory systems will fall upon hard times if the citizenry fails to place pressure—and, if necessary, electoral punishment—on those state office seekers and officeholders who abuse the public trust.

State campaign money does not exist in a vacuum, either, isolated from spending at the federal or local levels. In presidential campaigns, as noted, soft money has been a controversial factor. Often soft money goes unregulated because the states do not regulate uniformly amounts contributed or spent, nor is disclosure certain or timely. While soft money in presidential or congressional campaigns may emanate from national party origins of collection and allocation, the way each state regulates its own political money has implications for soft money raised or spent within that state for federal campaigns.[4]

## Disclosure: The Cornerstone of Campaign Finance Reform

Basic truths aside, there is at least one policy that should be universal in campaign finance regulation: comprehensive and timely disclosure. Regarded as a radical notion a generation ago, this policy is now considered fundamental to the political system by both liberals and conservatives. Today, arguing that the public does not have the right to know the sources from which candidates draw their money is akin to arguing that universal suffrage is not such a great idea.

Disclosure laws make it difficult for a political figure to claim, ex post facto, that an ill-gotten personal gain was meant really to be a legal campaign contribution. In recent years, prosecutions of elected officials on corruption charges have relied increasingly on information—or the absence of information— filed in campaign reports.

Unfortunately, while all fifty states have disclosure laws on the books (see Appendix 2A), they vary in quality and are implemented unevenly. In several states, reports for legislative candidates are filed only at the local level, with no requirement that a copy of the report be forwarded to a central repository at the state capital. In some states, campaign disclosure reports are available for inspection only during limited hours, and charges to photocopy them are inordinately high. In South Carolina, one of two states that still lacks preelection disclosure, postelection reports for legislative candidates are filed with legislative ethics committees rather than with the State Ethics Commission. Those wishing to inspect the legislative disclosure forms are then required to make an appointment with the House or Senate committee.[5]

At the very least, reports should be made available during regular office hours, and public photocopying fees should not exceed the cost to the office in question. The North Carolina Center for Public Policy Research undertook a study of disclosure laws in the fifty states and used the information as the basis for recommendations, released in March 1990, for improving the North Carolina system.[6] Although some are debatable, they are at least worth consideration by other states as well:

❏ All candidates for statewide and state legislative office should have to file with the state election agency, rather than allowing legislative aspirants to file only at their local board. If all candidates filed with the state as well as the local election agency, the reports would be easily accessible to the public, the study noted.

❏ Reports should include the occupation and principal place of employment of contributors, so as to allow the public to see which financial interests are supporting a candidate, party, or PAC. This requirement has been part of federal law for twenty years but is absent from disclosure laws in a number of states.

❏ Penalties for those not filing reports should be set at $1,000 for candidates and $5,000 for committees, along with the possibility of time in prison. The North Carolina group also said the names of nonfilers and those filing late should be made readily available for publication in the media, and that those who intentionally misreport information should face possible forfeiture of the nomination or election.

A system of campaign disclosure for candidates will accomplish only a fraction of the job if it is not accompanied by financial disclosure by officeholders, in which they declare their personal holdings as well as speaking fees and gifts from those seeking to influence policy. Finally, given the Supreme Court's decision that spending limits on independent expenditures are unconstitutional, disclosure is one of the few means of restraining these often-negative campaigns.

But disclosure is only a start in achieving effective campaign finance regulation. Writing in 1976, David Broder, one of the nation's leading political journalists, commented: "Disclosure . . . may be a necessary ingredient in an effective strategy against the corrupting influence of money on politics, but it is not sufficient to guarantee against impropriety. Its chief advantage is that it focuses press and public attention on the candidates' actual or potential conflicts of interest. Its drawback is that it does not, by itself, seem to insulate the candidate from those influences."[7] Judging from the frequent scandal and subterfuge that has plagued the campaign finance system during the past decade, Broder's observation was on the mark.

## Election Agencies: Giving the Watchdog Some Independence

As with disclosure, a strong election agency alone cannot prevent candidates and officeholders from choosing expediency over propriety in certain situations. Ultimately, a seeker of elective office must decide if it is in his or her self-interest to behave in an ethical manner. This decision can be influenced through a series of positive incentives like public funding—to be discussed in detail later—and negative incentives, such as the willingness of the public to toss out errant public servants. An election agency can play an important role when it comes to exacting punishment for lawbreaking. If it pursues evidence of impropriety aggressively and is unafraid to bring charges when there is wrongdoing, it will help the voting public to decide which officials are worthy of their continued trust.

A note of caution is necessary here. Just as too little money in the political system can be as harmful as too much, so can too much regulation by an independent election commission do as much damage as not enough. If a paucity of regulation can shake public confidence in the system, an overabundance of it can stifle spontaneity on the campaign trail and diminish the amount and quality of information available to the public. The voters, to say nothing of the First Amendment, are hardly served when candidates begin to censor themselves for fear of running afoul of the mandates of an overzealous commission. Laws should not lead commissions into a posture of micromanagement of political campaigns.

To date, however, it appears that the primary problem has been that of underregulation rather than overregulation. While a bare majority of states now have established election commissions to oversee disclosure and enforce other campaign-finance-related statutes, even the best of these agencies suffer from insufficient funding and inadequate enforcement powers. Some do not even have the resources to compile and analyze the campaign finance reports submitted by candidates. Such studies are an integral part of any effective disclosure law.

To some extent, election commissions have been victims of the same across-the-board cuts as other agencies, as state governments tighten their belts in lean economic times. But whatever the health of the state treasury, there is an inherent conflict of interest in election commissions depending on the generosity of the people whom they regulate. If a state legislator has been cited by a commission for running afoul of the election laws, how magnanimous is he expected to be when the commission's annual budget request comes along? Conversely, can commissions be expected to pursue vigorously allegations of wrongdoing when the path may lead to those that hold the purse strings?

Such concerns hold true at the local level as well as state and federal levels, as evidenced in a 1989 report by the California Commission on Campaign Financing. The report, *Money and Politics in the Golden State: Financing California's Local Elections*, said that district attorneys, city attorneys, and elections officials are often reluctant to enforce relevant laws because mayors, city councils, and boards of supervisors control their budgets.[8]

Among those singled out for criticism was the Los Angeles city clerk, Elias Martinez, who is appointed by the mayor and confirmed by the city council. Martinez, criticized by the commission for delaying investigations of allegations against two members of the city council, welcomed the CCCF's recommendation for an independent commission to enforce campaign laws. "The city clerks are put in a tough position when they have to fine council members," Martinez told the *Los Angeles Times*. "I fined a couple of council and those kinds of things do not endear you to council members who determine your pay. It definitely impacted on me on my merit pay."[9]

Given the inevitability of conflict of interest, there is a case to be made for providing election agencies with a source of funding independent of the normal legislative appropriations process. California's Fair

Political Practices Commission is the one state agency that enjoys this independence (for half its current funding); despite this, the FPPC has had to reduce its monthly newsletter to a bimonthly, and to cut back on educational seminars and workshops. New Jersey has taken a small step in this direction by dedicating all election-related fines to the work of the state's Election Law Enforcement Commission.

## Contribution Limits: Striking a Balance

The late senator Lee Metcalf of Montana, in discussing the Federal Election Campaign Act, once wondered aloud whether officeholders should not worry about serving time rather than serving their constituents. His quip neatly summarizes the constant tension that exists in campaign reform between preventing and penalizing abuses and protecting constitutional rights. It also suggests a complaint of many of today's politicians: that the media and the public usually hold them to be guilty until they are proven innocent.

While this paper has cited several cases in which elected officials have been formally charged with wrongdoing, they are the exception rather than the rule. Far more common is the situation in which large contributions from a single individual or organization have created perceived impropriety rather than actual violations of the law. That distinction is not intended to belittle the problem. Widespread public perception of corruption is a reality that undermines the very legitimacy of the political system. As the recent report of a symposium of state legislators noted:

> The statehouse press corps is of the belief that campaign contributions affect the legislative process. . . . Whether that is actually the case or not, there can be little doubt that the press and the public perceive that legislators and legislatures are being corrupted by campaign contributions. Even those who defend current practices admit that money presents problems.[10]

Clearly, the way to greater public trust of elected representatives involves setting contribution limits that strike a balance between the need to reduce perceptions of corruption and the need for office seekers to communicate effectively with the voting electorate. The limits in any given state must bear a relationship to the costs of campaigning. For example, contribution limits arguably need to be set higher in densely populated New Jersey—where candidates seeking to purchase television time must do so in the highly expensive New York and Philadelphia markets—than in sparsely populated Great Plains states, where television time remains a relative bargain. Likewise, if a state's geography and political folkways have nurtured a tradition of low-cost, personal one-on-one campaigning, a low limit on contributions will ensure clean politics without circumscribing a candidate's ability to campaign. If, however, there is a tradition of high-cost, electronic campaigning, setting a low contribution limit will tend to work to the advantage of incumbents, who are better known than their opponents and frequently more experienced in the subtleties of politicking.

The lowest state contribution limit is in Arizona, with an indexed total in mid-1991 of $610 per election cycle for the primary and general election combined. This is lower than Florida's newly legislated level of $500 per election. In Arizona, although political parties can register as super-PACs and then contribute up to $3,040, neither major party has done so. Such low limits on parties as well as individuals seem intended to starve candidates financially, and require them to spend more time fund-raising. Florida, due to its public financing program, can keep in check candidates' self-contributions, but Arizona, with its stricter limits may actually give an advantage to wealthy candidates. Limits on contributions should be reasonably high, calibrated to campaign needs in states where television or direct mail are expensive, and sufficient to ensure that the voting public will be well informed.

Otherwise, contribution limits may trigger independent expenditures. Although expenditure limits often are blamed as the most important cause of independent expenditures, in California, for example, independent expenditures were mainly made in connection with ballot measures until Proposition 73 introduced limits on contributions to candidates. In legislative campaigns, independent expenditures were only $27,494 in 1988 but jumped to $1.8 million in 1990, following the imposition of a $1,000 contribution limit. In 1990, $748,221 was spent independently on behalf of gubernatorial candidate Pete Wilson. Total 1990 independent expenditures in California campaigns were almost $4 million, with only contribution limits—not expenditure limits—to spark their spending.[11]

Building up a sizable donor base without relying on the support of the wealthy takes time, and an excessively low contribution limit can therefore have an adverse impact on the attention incumbents give to the job to which they were elected. At the federal level, there are continual complaints from congressional leaders that the rank and file are so busy fund-raising that they have less and less time to devote to legislating. It should be noted that the federal limits on individual and PAC contributions ($1,000 and $5,000 respectively) have not been raised since their adoption in 1974. But inflation over the past decade and a half has reduced the real value of these amounts by almost two-thirds.

Obviously, this is not to suggest a return to the days when a congressional candidate could line up campaign funding by making a few phone calls to five- and six-figure contributors. A large donor base consisting of many small contributors can help to reduce public cynicism. But direct mail fund-raising is expensive and adds to campaign costs. At the same time, when a state or local legislature determines a fair contribution limit, it should be indexed to the cost of living and rounded to the nearest hundred dollars, so that elected officials do not become full-time fund-raisers constantly chasing additions to their donor lists.

The rationale for setting contribution limits should apply across-the-board, to corporations, labor unions, and PACs as well as individual donations. At present, the ceilings adopted by the various states display little consistency or internal logic (see Appendix 2A). A number of states that prohibit or limit corporate contributions permit unlimited donations by unions, a tribute to the past or present clout of labor. Yet other states restrict corporate or union contributions only to permit such money to flow into the system in the form of unlimited contributions from corporate or labor PACs.

To the greatest extent possible, donations from labor unions and corporations—as well as banks—should be treated alike; there is little ground for discriminating among them. A case can be made for banning both. Unlike PACs, which draw their money from voluntary contributions knowingly made for political purposes, direct union and corporate donations represent an involuntary political donation drawn from stockholders' profits or union members' dues.

In contrast to prohibitions of corporate or labor contributions, no state has successfully banned PAC donations outright, and few have even tried. Legal opinions widely hold that such an attempt would run into constitutional problems, as it did in Connecticut. Looking at the issue from a strictly pragmatic standpoint, any effort to do away with PACs would likely create more problems than it would solve. A ban on PACs would produce a result similar to limits on overall spending: accelerated use of such controversial channels as independent expenditures and soft money. These forms of political finance are far harder to track for purposes of disclosure than PAC donations.

Acceptance of this reality is not meant to minimize the problems of perception and public confidence caused by the increasing amounts of PAC money flowing into state legislative campaigns. Limits on PAC donations are just one of several steps needed to clean up the image of campaigning. Clearly, such limits are both constitutional and desirable in terms of policy. Restrictions should be across-the-board and easily enforceable by the proper authority. At both the federal and state levels, there have been proposals to allow PACs with large memberships to contribute more than those with small memberships; Arizona and California have made such distinctions into law. The problem with this approach, besides adding unnecessary complexity to the regulatory system, is that it definitely favors labor unions, professional associations, and perhaps environmental groups, which comprise a majority of the large-member PACs.

One type of spending has persistently frustrated attempts to control campaign contributions: the ever-increasing amounts of corporate and union money funneled into initiatives and referenda in states where these devices are permitted. Under Supreme Court rulings, there is nothing that can be done to limit such contributions.[12] The problem has been most acute in California, the longtime king of the ballot initiative. In 1988, an astounding $140 million was spent in the Golden State to pass or defeat statewide ballot propositions. The largest chunk, $84 million, was spent on a battle over insurance rate reductions; $64 million of that came from the insurance industry.[13] The California insurance battle was by far the most expensive statewide campaign in U.S. history. Unless the high court changes its mind, ballot measures will continue to be a large component of political spending.

## Aggregate Limits

Political action committee activity has risen dramatically in recent years in most of the states, and attempting to limit the role of PACs in the election process has been one of the chief concerns of political reformers. Legislation to abolish PACs has been discussed in several states but, as noted, probably would be invalidated on constitutional grounds. There is a far greater likelihood that states will attempt to place limitations on PAC influence, as Wisconsin has done, by limiting the aggregate amount candidates may accept from political action committees. Arizona, Hawaii, Kansas, and Montana also have had aggregate limits, and in 1989 Louisiana added itself to the list.

However, as with efforts to do away with PACs altogether, proposals to place an aggregate limit on PAC contributions suffer from potential constitutional as well as practical problems. Notwithstanding the Supreme Court's recent refusal to hear the Gard case from Wisconsin (see Chapter 3), there remains concern in legal circles over whether aggregate contribution limits are consistent with the Court's 1976 decision in *Buckley v. Valeo*. According to this view, aggregate limits on contributions—by restricting total donations from certain sources available to a candidate—serve as de facto spending ceilings, in contravention of the Supreme Court finding that spending limits are unconstitutional unless accepted voluntarily in return for an inducement such as public financing.

"Aggregate contribution limits restrict campaign spending to a much greater degree than normal contribution limits," Don M. Millis contended in a 1989 *Wisconsin Law Review* article on that state's regulatory system. "When a candidate reaches the Interest PAC aggregate contribution limit, an entire class of funds (i.e. Interest PAC contributions) is unavailable to that candidate."

He continued, "When a candidate reaches the normal contribution limit for a single Interest PAC or single individual, that candidate is only precluded from receiving more funds from a particular Interest PAC or individual. In most cases, there will still be hundreds of potential Interest PAC contributors and thousands of potential contributors from which funds can be tapped."[14]

Arguably, aggregate limits put a ceiling on contributions rather than expenditures, and therefore constitutional considerations may be less compelling.[15] But legal theory aside, they have yielded some unpleasant side effects in the states where they have been adopted. In Wisconsin, limits on PAC contributions have given rise to increased use of "conduit" contributions, which disguise interest group funding as individual donations.

Between 1986 and 1988, contributions from so-called regulated conduits jumped 47 percent in Wisconsin.[16] And that does not count other types of conduit contributions that remain unregulated because of a loophole in the law. Millis writes, "To the degree that aggregate limits on Interest PAC contributions encourage covert conduit contributions, the goal of public disclosure is defeated. Pledge conduit managers can funnel thousands of dollars to candidates without public awareness that what appears to be a large number of individual contributions actually represents an orchestrated effort by a special interest group."[17]

Meanwhile, in Arizona, a 1986 initiative imposing aggregate limits resulted in a 23 percent drop in contributions to winning legislative candidates in the 1988 elections.[18] But independent expenditures rose to an estimated $1 million, due in part to campaigns organized by the business community. The independent expenditure campaigns even included reproduced endorsements of candidates by other candidates. Although the Arizona experience shows that aggregate limits can force down PAC spending, the policy consideration is whether the accompanying rise in independent expenditures is desirable.

## Public Funding: The Search for the Ideal System

Public funding is the one major element of campaign finance that offers positive rather than negative reinforcement; it provides an incentive for candidates who act in a preferred manner under conditions set forth by the government. In that sense, it is cost-effective to the taxpayers, notwithstanding the significant outlay of public money required for success.

But there are rewards for the candidate as well as the voting public. The need for the candidate to seek less than desirable sources of private funding is reduced, thereby diminishing the negative perception that such a money chase creates. It presumably allows the candidate to spend more time communicating with the public, rather than trying to squeeze in campaigning between hours on the phone cajoling donors.

The public not only gets more of the candidate's time, but also gains leverage over the candidate. In New Jersey, for example, acceptance of public funding compels a candidate to agree to a number of debates with his or her opponents, an idea now being promoted in Congress for future publicly funded presidential elections. In Wisconsin, a candidate who accepts public financing loses a dollar of his or her subsidy for every dollar received in PAC contributions.

Given the Supreme Court's 1976 *Buckley v. Valeo* decision, public financing or other incentives are necessary if a candidate is to agree to limit the amount of campaign spending or of personal resources used. Public financing with conditions attached, advocates argue, can "level the playing field" by neutralizing the advantages of wealthy candidates, or those with more campaign money. Of course, wealthy candidates may refuse the public funding and not be bound by the spending limits.

None of this is to suggest that public financing is universally embraced. From a fiscal standpoint, there are those who feel that it is an inappropriate use of scarce government dollars in what has been traditionally a private-sector activity. From a philosophical standpoint, others think that it places too much control over the elective process by those already in power and interested in staying there. Nonetheless, public financing of candidates and parties is slowly winning wider acceptance at both the state and local levels. (See Appendix 1 and Appendix 3.) Almost half the states now provide some form of it.

Unfortunately, public funding schemes have not always worked as well as they could. Some suffer from a lack of resources. Some have attempted to spread the money too thin. Yet others suffer from flawed structures. In order to succeed, public funding must be considered as the main alternative source of funding for political candidates. That means, above all, the system has to be adequately funded.

If, as in most existing systems, a candidate is compelled to accept expenditure limits in return for public financing, he or she must receive a large enough grant to make it worthwhile to limit spending. Otherwise, as in the Hawaii situation detailed in Chapter 2, public funding will attract few participants. Alternatively, if a state or locality opts for the "floors without ceiling" approach—in which a candidate is given "seed money" without having to abide by a spending ceiling—ample funding is still necessary for the candidate to be able to afford to make a case to the voters.

Two other points are worth considering. In the case of New Jersey, where expensive media markets in New York City and Philadelphia are necessary to gubernatorial campaigns, public financing amounts to a transfer of funds from New Jersey taxpayers to out-of-state broadcasters.

In recent years there has been an increase in negative campaigning. Whatever the effectiveness as a strategy, negativity turns off many voters. Taxpayers may not want to support such campaigning with their tax dollars. Negative campaigning will be utilized regardless of whether campaigns are publicly financed, but adherents of public financing should recognize the danger signal, which already may be apparent in the decrease in tax checkoff rates.

## Expenditure Ceilings: Do They Work?

When it comes to political finance reform, no issue has been as controversial as spending limits. At the federal level, a partisan stalemate over this question has held up efforts to amend the Federal Election Campaign Act for a decade.

While spending limitations can be shown to be illusory, ineffective, and even damaging to competition, concern about high campaign costs has led some states to seek their enactment. The problem with expenditure limits is that they reduce flexibility and rigidify the campaign process while inviting less accountable ways of spending, such as independent expenditures, issue campaigns related to the candidates' positions, and soft money.

Proponents argue that such ceilings are the only way to hold down the rising costs of campaigns and prevent qualified candidates of modest means from being priced out of the market. They say that contribution limits are not sufficient to do this; candidates will simply chase more contributions and continue spending. As a practical political matter, legislatures are reluctant to provide public dollars for campaigns with the sky the limit. Why give public money, they ask, and then leave the candidate free to seek as much private funding as desired?

But it should be noted that in New Jersey—the state with perhaps the greatest experience in implementing gubernatorial public financing—the Election Law Enforcement Commission has recommended three times that expenditure ceilings be repealed. New Jersey illustrates two of the biggest problems with these limits: the advantage they confer on incumbents and their virtual unenforceability.

ELEC first recommended doing away with the ceilings after the 1977 gubernatorial election when they put a challenger at a significant disadvantage against the better-known incumbent. In 1989, there is evidence to suggest that, despite the action by the legislature to raise the spending ceilings significantly, both Democrats and Republicans found so many ways around them as to render them all but meaningless. The New Jersey experience, along with that of public financing at the presidential level, also serves to demonstrate that ceilings often simply transfer special interest money into hard-to-trace channels such as independent expenditures and soft money.

Yet another undesirable effect of spending ceilings is to encourage even more "negative campaigning" at a time when opinion polls reflect increasing public cynicism toward the political process. While voters often disdain such tactics in the abstract, negative campaigns persist because they have been shown to sway voter opinion in many instances. A candidate operating under spending ceilings likely will be more inclined to "go negative," since that type of tactic is a lot more cost-effective than loftier forms of campaigning. A negative advertising barrage can quickly drive up an opponent's disapproval ratings, allowing the attacker to maximize the effect of his or her ability to use campaign cash under the limit.

To place limits on spending is to argue that campaigns cost too much. But how does one determine empirically how much is too much? And at what cost in terms of free speech? While few are happy with the thirty-second, frequently negative television spots omnipresent in today's campaigns, spending limitations provide no solution, stifling political dialogue rather than expanding it. The result will be fewer truly competitive races. Why not take a more expansive outlook, that elections are improved by well-financed candidates able to wage competitive campaigns? This point of view gets too little acceptance in an atmosphere decrying high costs.

Massachusetts is one of the few states to have implemented a "floors without ceilings" system, which distributed more than $865,000 in 1986 to candidates without forcing them to abide by spending limits. That relatively modest investment nevertheless produced some significant results in weaning candidates from dependence on private contributions. The Democratic candidate for attorney general financed more than 13 percent of his campaign with public money; his Republican opponent underwrote almost a quarter of his campaign budget with public funds. And, while Democratic governor Michael Dukakis—then gearing up for a presidential campaign—financed only 4 percent of his campaign with taxpayer funds, the comparable figure for his Republican opponent was more than 30 percent.[19]

While the preferable course is to eschew spending limits, those states that feel compelled to impose them would do well to follow the advice of the model campaign statute recently unveiled by COGEL. According to the model's drafters: "The size of the limits is a critical decision. The expenditure limits should be set high enough to ensure a full presentation and discussion of the issues. The actual amount will vary considerably dependent on the circumstances unique to the jurisdiction."[20] Spending ceilings and allocations of public funding, like contribution limits, should be indexed for inflation. In Minnesota, candidate participation fell when the ceilings were not indexed for inflation, and then rose when the legislature allowed for increasing costs to be taken into account.

Minnesota, among the most innovative states when it comes to campaign reform, in 1987 adopted a provision under which a candidate who accepts public funding does not have to abide by the state's spending limits if his or her opponent declines to accept public funding. Wisconsin has a similar provision. As with Minnesota's recent attempt to impose state public financing on federal elections, it remains to be seen whether this approach ultimately holds up under judicial scrutiny. Penalizing candidates for not accepting public money contains an element of coercion that may run counter to the basis of the Supreme Court's *Buckley* decision.

## Raising the Public Money

Fifteen years ago, David Broder wrote, "It is clear, unhappily, that few of the voters who are quick to complain about politicians 'selling out' to their contributors are themselves ready to put money into the political process."[21] In the intervening years, that problem has gotten worse rather than better.

New Jersey, the state where taxpayers have been the most supportive of public funding, has seen public participation in the income tax checkoff drop by 20 percent since 1980. In Michigan, participation in the tax checkoff has dropped by 50 percent over the past decade. While polls sometimes show that the voters support public funding in the abstract, it seems that they cannot overcome a general distrust of public subsidies to politicians when it comes time to exercise their option as taxpayers to check off a dollar or so.

In the face of these trends, legislatures face several options if they are to keep public financing systems viable:

### Increasing the Checkoff

In Minnesota, the checkoff was raised from one dollar to five at a time when participation in the checkoff had fallen by a third. Interestingly, the participation rate showed little decline when the checkoff was raised to five dollars in 1987, and the total sum raised through the checkoff more than doubled.[22] Rhode Island also has a five-dollar checkoff.

### Using the Legislative Appropriations Process

New Jersey currently takes this approach. Money from the tax checkoff is directed to the general fund, and the legislature then appropriates the money needed to implement public funding, in effect making up the difference between the amount collected by the checkoff and the cost of the program. The problem with relying on legislative appropriations rather than solely a checkoff or other dedicated funds is that what the legislature giveth it can taketh away. An example is Florida, where the legislature in 1986 appropriated $3 million for public funding, only to rescind the move several months later in the face of a tight state budget; it took five years subsequently for Florida to enact a sustainable public financing program.

### Educating the Public

In 1988, the Wisconsin legislature voted to fund a statewide educational program to encourage taxpayers to use the checkoff, but the measure was vetoed by Governor Tommy Thompson. A year earlier, Common Cause of Wisconsin tested an education program in four counties involving public service spots and brochures. Participation increased 2 percent in these areas.[23] If public funding systems are to thrive, there is a growing consensus that states must be willing to do more to educate the taxpayers than simply placing a brief informational statement inside tax forms.

There also is the issue of competition from "add-ons" benefiting a variety of state programs. While checkoffs do not increase one's tax liability and add-ons do, there has nevertheless been a decline in the political funding checkoff in several states when competing add-ons have appeared on the tax form.[24] It is clear that political funding does not have the same appeal to taxpayers as, say, protecting wildlife. If state election campaigns are to remain adequately funded, it may be desirable for states to restrict the use of competing tax add-ons.

While they do not qualify as public funding per se, tax credits and deductions to encourage small donations to candidates from rank-and-file citizens have been employed by various states over the years. By the mid-1980s, eighteen states offered an incentive along this line, some indirectly through the effects of the federal tax credit. But the federal government's tax overhaul legislation in 1986 did away with the tax credit for political donations, and a number of states then moved to make their tax structure consistent with the federal one. Today, only seven states still make use of tax sweeteners for small contributions.

There is now discussion in Congress of restoring the federal tax credit for donations, and if that were enacted it might prompt several states to follow suit. The drawback is that it represents a drain on state treasuries at a time when most have severe budgetary problems. In any case, evidence is inconclusive as to whether such credits prod people who otherwise would not have made political contributions to participate in the campaign finance system.

## Allocating the Public Money

Of the four states that have featured major public financing programs in recent years, New Jersey and Michigan have concentrated on funding gubernatorial races, while Minnesota and Wisconsin have funded numerous statewide offices as well as legislative races. A case can be made for focusing limited resources on the governorship, in that it is the most important statewide office. In fact, in New Jersey the governor is the only statewide elected official and has the power to appoint the cabinet officers, including the attorney general and state treasurer.

The other side of this argument is that those running for governor are highly visible candidates who are in a position to attract the most desirable kind of private money: small donations from a broad base of donors. That is not the case with relatively unknown state legislators. "The housewife or electrician or small businessman who has a desire to serve in the legislature will not . . . get much help from his party or from her neighbors in financing a race," David Broder wrote in the mid-1970s. "If the candidate is able to get money at all (which is not likely if an incumbent is the opponent) it will come from the highway builders, or the liquor dealers, or the public employees' union or some other group . . . which has a direct interest in how that candidate will vote on issues vital to its economic well-being."[25]

That is precisely what has happened in New Jersey in recent years: much of the special interest money is being attracted into legislative contests. PAC money is becoming a staple in legislative races around the country. However, trying to cover too many races with too little money may undermine public funding. In Wisconsin, with available amounts of public funding on the decline, participation by legislative candidates dropped significantly from 1986 to 1988. Decisions must be made on a state-by-state basis, contingent on the willingness of the legislature and the public to provide tax dollars.

**There are several other significant distribution issues:**

❏ Ideally, public funding should be extended to primaries as well as general elections. To limit it to general elections is simply to encourage special interest money to flow into the primary. Wisconsin has tried to get around this problem by mandating that any candidate who accepts public funds must live by spending limits in both the primary and general election, even though the state makes funds available only for the general election. This strategy is not only inequitable but also constitutionally questionable. It amounts to a mandatory expenditure ceiling in the primary, and *Buckley v. Valeo* allows only for ceilings accepted voluntarily in return for incentives. To date, however, there has been no legal challenge to this provision, which the Wisconsin attorney general ruled to be constitutional more than a decade ago.[26]

❏ Very few observers favor total state-supported funding of election campaigns. A mixture that includes some private funding, raised in small donations, is considered desirable to demonstrate that a candidate has a base of support before he or she receives public money.

❏ Once a candidate has secured the party's nomination, a flat grant of public funding is preferable to the "matching fund" approach often used in primaries. Because many primaries are held late—August and September—it gives a candidate little time to raise private funds for the general election that can be matched by public money. Consequently, the matching fund system can put candidates in a cash flow squeeze at a time when they may have to buy television time and make other commitments for the general election campaign.

❏ In allocating public funding, perhaps the most basic question is: Should it be minimal in the form of seed money to help candidates get their campaigns started, or should it be extensive—to cover basic campaign costs? The answer depends upon whether public funding is designed to be the desired alternative in those jurisdictions that choose to limit private donations by means of low contribution or aggregate limits, or whether it is intended merely as a "start-up" fund to encourage candidates who otherwise would forgo a campaign out of financial concerns.

## Public Funding and Political Parties

Recent years have witnessed an outpouring of nostalgia for the faded political party. Not everyone shares that feeling. After all, the arrival of public financing in New Jersey was in large measure a response to corruption spawned by a handful of urban political machines whose leaders all but ran the state for decades. But parties are unlikely to ever achieve that kind of clout again, largely because the electronic age has enabled aspiring politicians to run around them rather than rise through them.

The decline of party discipline has allowed an egocentric attitude to pervade state legislatures as well as Congress. Often, the tangle of competing incumbent self-interest leads to political paralysis on important policy issues. Parties, it is frequently argued, with broader interests and a broader donor base, represent a less corrupting influence than many of the sources of money that have supplanted them in recent years. Consequently, strengthening political parties can bring about cleaner as well as more efficient government. Parties offer a way to wean candidates away from PAC contributions to the extent that parties are able to raise the money, or receive it from state tax checkoffs or add-ons, to help support candidates running on the party ticket.

A number of states have been innovative in their support of political parties through income tax checkoffs and add-ons. Party committees in these states have come to depend on public funding. For example, in Kentucky, where the tax checkoff is operative, in a six-month period in 1988–89, the state Democratic central committee received $110,500 in designated tax funds, or 33 percent of its income. The Republican committee took in $69,800, or 45 percent.[27] Additional amounts go to county committees. While the proceeds do not always go directly to candidates, the party-building activities thus paid for are of assistance to candidates.

At present, the role once played by the parties—discipline—has been taken over increasingly by so-called leadership PACs created by leading members of state legislatures. They provide funding to party candidates and collect chits in return. Often, however, their agenda is not the broad one advanced by a political party but a narrow one focused on their own ambition and self- advancement. It would therefore be preferable to funnel money to candidates through parties rather than these leadership PACs.

But parties must not be allowed to become laundering operations for unlimited donations from corporations, labor unions, and PACs. Otherwise, the perception of corruption by the general public will change little. New Jersey's Ad Hoc Commission on Legislative Ethics and Campaign Finance wisely recommended that contributions from any corporation, union, or PAC to state political parties be limited to $25,000 annually. "The . . . limit will restrict the potential influence over the party of any one contributor or group of contributors."[28] In other states, a different limit may be more appropriate.

States giving financial assistance to political parties help to strengthen the party system, reduce candidates' dependence on wealthy colleagues and PAC-supported legislative leaders, and may lessen the need for expensive outside consultants to the extent the parties' funding or services help candidates directly. Strengthened parties more easily facilitate the creation of the coalitions and voting blocs that are essential to democratic government; they increase accountability by holding elected officials responsible for their performances.[29]

## Looking Ahead

In the late 1970s, the initiative for change in the area of campaign finance reform passed from reformers and their allies in the media to candidates, officeholders, parties, and interest groups—those most directly affected by the reform laws. For a time in the early 1980s, election reform appeared comatose.

The mid- to late 1980s witnessed a renaissance for reform at the state and local levels. One of the challenges for state and local legislatures, as they confront the decade of the 1990s, is to maintain that momentum despite budgetary constraints. As Steve Johnson, an Indiana legislator, recently cautioned his colleagues from other states, "The more careerist and more professionalized we become, the more we tend to look at this re-election concept and want to continue in this career, so we don't take risks. Therefore, the notion of states as laboratories begins to diminish."[30]

With state legislatures now undertaking another census reapportionment, the professionalization of which Johnson speaks will unquestionably intensify efforts by incumbents to emerge from the decennial maneuvering with safe seats intact. The reapportionment issue cannot be divorced from political finance reform, which strives to ensure competitive elections in the face of the increasing fund-raising advantages enjoyed by incumbents.

The 1980s saw setbacks as well as succeses in election reform. For all the states and municipalities that have made strides, there remain many where relatively little has changed in the past two decades.

What is universal is the nationwide focus on campaign finance reform: it is being debated in states as diverse as California, where state Senate districts are larger than U.S. House districts, and New Hampshire, where a delegate to the lower house of the legislature represents only 2,500 constituents.

It is more than coincidence that this debate has intensified at a time when several state legislatures have suffered through the ignominy of widespread corruption probes, driving down public trust in state and local government. In California, once considered home to a model legislature, a recent *Los Angeles Times* poll found that a majority of voters believe the taking of bribes to be a common practice in the state legislature. Public officials across the country who choose to ignore such perceptions do so at the risk of permitting further erosion of confidence in the electoral process.

# Notes

## Introduction

1. Ruth S. Jones, "A Decade of U.S. State-level Campaign Finance Reform," paper presented at the Roundtable on Political Finance and Political Corruption of the International Political Science Association, sponsored by the Institute for Political Studies in Japan, Tokyo, September 1989, p. 3.

2. Estimates by the Citizens' Research Foundation, Los Angeles, put 1988 spending for statewide and state legislative office at $540 million and $365 million for local office. Cited in Herbert E. Alexander and Monica Bauer, *Financing the 1988 Election* (Boulder, Colo.: Westview Press, 1991), pp. 2–5.

3. Sandra J. Singer, "The Arms Race of Campaign Financing," *State Legislatures,* July 1988, p. 24.

4. Sandra J. Singer, "The Power of the Purse—It Costs to Run for Legislative Office!!" paper presented at the Western Political Science Association annual meeting, Salt Lake City, March 30–April 1, 1989, p. 5.

## Chapter 1

1. *The New Gold Rush: Financing California's Legislative Campaigns,* report and recommendations of the California Commission on Campaign Financing (Los Angeles: Center for Responsive Government, 1985), p. 1.

2. *The New Gold Rush,* 1987 update, p. 9.

3. Frank J. Sorauf, *Money in American Elections* (Glenview, Ill.: Scott, Foresman and Company, 1988), p. 266.

4. "Spending by Senate Legislative Candidates Hits New Record in 1988," report by California Common Cause, Los Angeles, February 16, 1989, p. 103.

5. Sandra J. Singer, "The Power of the Purse—It Costs to Run for Legislative Office!!" paper presented at the Western Political Science Association annual meeting, Salt Lake City, March 30–April 1, 1989, pp. 7–8.

6. Gary Moncrief, "The Increase in Campaign Expenditures in State Legislative Elections: A Comparison of Four Northwestern States," paper presented at the American Political Science Association annual meeting, San Francisco, August 30–September 2, 1990, p. 2.

7. Ruth S. Jones, "Financing State Elections," in *Money and Politics in the United States: Financing Elections in the 1980s,* ed. Michael J. Malbin (Chatham, N.J.: Chatham House Publishers, 1984), p. 208.

8. Herbert E. Alexander and Monica Bauer, *Financing the 1988 Election* (Boulder, Colo.: Westview Press, 1991), p. 4.

9. Singer, "The Power of the Purse," p. 4.

10. Sandra J. Singer, "The Arms Race of Campaign Financing," *State Legislatures,* July 1988, p. 28.

11. Moncrief, "The Increase in Campaign Expenditures in State Legislative Elections," p. 12.

12. Thad Beyle, "Governor's Chair Now Costs $7 Million," *State Government News*, The Council of State Governments, Lexington, Ky., October 1986, p. 21.

13. Penny Miller, "Costs of State Races Have Increased Dramatically," *The Kentucky Journal*, Lexington, July 1990, pp. 15–16.

14. Data provided by Professor Thad Beyle of the University of North Carolina, from a forthcoming article in *State Government News*, The Council of State Governments, Lexington, Ky., November 1991.

15. Carol Matlack, "Elections You Can Afford," *National Journal*, June 24, 1989, p. 1633.

16. Ibid.

17. George Skelton, "Legislators on the Take, Most in Survey Believe," *Los Angeles Times,* January 3, 1990.

18. "Findings and Recommendations of the Ad Hoc Commission on Legislative Ethics and Campaign Finance: A Report to the President of the Senate, Speaker of the General Assembly and Members of the New Jersey Legislature," Trenton, October 22, 1990, p. 3.

19. *Campaign Finance Law 90* (Washington, D.C.: National Clearinghouse on Election Administration, Federal Election Commission, 1990). This biennial publication contains a comprehensive summary of the laws of all fifty states.

20. Statement of John D. Feerick, chairman, New York Commission on Government Integrity, September 18, 1990. For a compilation of the work of the commission, see Bruce A. Green, ed., *Government Ethics Reform for the 1990s: The Collected Reports of the New York State Commission on Government Integrity*, part 1, "Campaign Financing" (New York: Fordham University Press, 1991), pp. 15–266.

21. Kent Jenkins, Jr., "$25 Million Race for Virginia Governor among Costliest," *Washington Post*, December 2, 1989.

22. Matlack, "Elections You Can Afford," p. 1634.

23. Ibid.

24. Thomas Heath and Donald P. Baker, "Coleman Lobbied for Developer in '84," *Washington Post*, October 19, 1989.

25. Kent Jenkins, Jr., "Developers' Money Fuels Race in Va.," *Washington Post*, October 8, 1989.

26. Kent Jenkins, Jr., "Wilder's Top Backer Puts $111,000 toward 'Jefferson's Concepts,'" *Washington Post*, August 28, 1989.

27. Donald P. Baker, "As Major Donor, McLean Developer Builds Hopes on Coleman," *Washington Post*, September 10, 1989.

28. Kent Jenkins, Jr., "Kluge Writes 2nd Check for $100,000 to Wilder," *Washington Post*, September 28, 1989.

29. Kent Jenkins, Jr., "Charlottesville Billionaires Planning Bash for Wilder," *Washington Post*, September 23, 1989.

30. Quoted in Jenkins, "Developers' Money Fuels Race in Va."

31. Moncrief, "The Increase in Campaign Expenditures in State Legislative Elections," p. 7.

32. Louis Peck, "Project 500 and the 1991 Initiative: The Party Committees Are Taking Aim at State Seats," *Campaigns & Elections*, January/February 1989, p. 15.

33. Quoted in ibid.

34. David Maraniss, "Texas, It Seems, Has Had Its Fill of Williams," *Washington Post*, October 27, 1990.

35. Quoted in David J. Heller, "Mail, Money and Machiavelli," *Campaigns & Elections*, November/December 1987, p. 34.

36. Joel Bradshaw and Elizabeth Sullivan, "The Case for Cooperation," *Campaigns & Elections*, March/April 1988, p. 60.

37. Ibid.

38. Moncrief, "The Increase in Campaign Expenditures in State Legislative Elections," p. 6.

39. *The New Gold Rush* (1985), p. 4.

40. Frank Lynn, "For Cuomo, Just Winning Won't Help a 1992 Bid," *The New York Times*, October 7, 1990.

41. Howard Schneider and Veronica T. Jennings, "Maryland's Gubernatorial Trail Diverges," *Washington Post*, October 30, 1990.

42. Estimates by Citizens' Research Foundation, Los Angeles.

43. Quoted in Jerry Hagstrom and Robert Guskind, "Mayoral Candidates Enter the Big Time Using Costly TV Ads and Consultants," *National Journal*, April 6, 1985, p. 738.

44. *Money and Politics in the Golden State: Financing California's Local Elections*, report and recommendations of the California Commission on Campaign Financing (Los Angeles: Center for Responsive Government, 1989), p. 1.

45. *The New Gold Rush* (1985), p. 6.

46. *The New Gold Rush* (1987), p. 17.

47. "PAC Money in Maryland: November 19, 1986–August 26, 1990," report available from Common Cause of Maryland, Annapolis, September 6, 1990, p. 1.

48. Ruth S. Jones, "A Decade of U.S. State-level Campaign Finance Reform," paper presented at the Roundtable on Political Finance and Political Corruption of the International Political Science Association, sponsored by the Institute for Political Studies in Japan, Tokyo, September 1989, p. 11.

49. Quoted in *The New Gold Rush* (1987), p. 19.

50. *Campaign Practices Reports*, 17, no. 21 (October 15, 1990): 7.

51. Quoted in Frank Lynn, "Regan Is Questioned on Fundraising," *The New York Times*, September 24, 1988.

52. Quoted in Paul Taylor, "Louisiana's Moveable Feast Flies to Paris to Retire Edwards Debt," *Washington Post*, January 20, 1984.

53. Daniel M. Weintraub and Richard C. Paddock, "Conviction Calls Capitol Practices into Doubt," *Los Angeles Times*, September 18, 1990.

54. Quoted in Walt Bogdanich, "In New York, Power of Real Estate Firms Comes under Scrutiny," *Wall Street Journal*, May 2, 1986.

55. Frank Clifford, "Political Donors Seeking an Ear," *Los Angeles Times*, March 11, 1985

56. *The New Gold Rush* (1985), p. 104.

57. *The New Gold Rush* (1987), p. 17.

58. Jones, "A Decade of U.S. State-level Campaign Finance Reform," p. 27.

59. Bob Paynter, Keith McKnight, and Andrew Zajac, "State Campaign Funds Masked in Pipeline," *Akron Beacon Journal*, October 1, 1989.

60. Keith McKnight and Andrew Zajac, "Dipping into Campaign Kitty," *Akron Beacon Journal*, September 23, 1990.

61. Common Cause, "PAC Money in Maryland," p. 1.

62. "The Golden Dome: A Study of Campaign Finance in 1988 Legislative Races," Common Cause of Massachusetts, Boston, October 23, 1989, p. iii.

63. "Incumbents Have Big Lead when It Comes to Business PAC Donations," *Los Angeles Times*, October 14, 1990.

64. *The New Gold Rush* (1987), p. 15.

65. Singer, "The Arms Race of Campaign Financing," p. 25.

66. *The New Gold Rush* (1987), p. 19.

67. Moncrief, "The Increase in Campaign Expenditures in State Legislative Elections," pp. 5–6.

68. Ibid., p. 8.

69. Jones, "A Decade of U.S. State-level Campaign Finance Reform," p. 2.

# Chapter 2

1. "Trends in Legislative Campaign Financing, 1977–87," white paper no. 2, New Jersey Election Law Enforcement Commission, Trenton, May 1989, pp. 48–49.

2. Jean Dykstra, "Feeding at the Campaign Trough," *New Jersey Reporter*, Princeton, February 1990, p. 9.

3. Ibid.

4. Robert Schwaneberg, "Lobbyist Sticks with 'Shakedown' Charge Despite Denial by Assemblymen," *Star-Ledger* (Newark), January 9, 1990.

5. Ibid.

6. Robert Schwaneberg, "State Continues Probe of Lobbyist Squeeze," *Star-Ledger* (Newark), February 11, 1991. Kotvas lost her job in September 1990, when LEGAL merged with another lobbying group.

7. Schwaneberg, "Lobbyist Sticks with 'Shakedown' Charge."

8. Kenny's predecessor was the legendary Frank Hague, who at the height of his power was mayor of Jersey City as well as chairman of both the Hudson County and New Jersey Democratic party. Despite his mere $7,500-a-year salary, Hague was reported to have been a multimillionaire at the time of his death in 1956.

9. Neal R. Peirce and Michael Barone, *The Mid-Atlantic States of America* (New York: W. W. Norton & Co., 1977), p. 219.

10. In 1972, Secretary of State Paul Sherwin—the closest political confidant of then governor William Cahill—was convicted of conspiring to influence highway contracts in return for contributions to the Republican State Finance Committee. The same year, Robert J. Burkhardt, who served as secretary of state in the late 1960s under Governor Richard J. Hughes, pled guilty to charges that—while running the Hughes reelection campaign in 1964–65—he demanded $20,000 from a construction firm to influence the contract for the second span of the Delaware Memorial Bridge. In 1973, former state treasurer John A. Kervick, regarded as the second most powerful man in the Hughes administration, pled guilty to fixing a highway contract while in office in return for kickbacks to the Democratic party. Meanwhile, J. M. McCrane, Cahill's state treasurer, was convicted of assisting corporations in disguising contributions to the Cahill campaign as tax-deductible expenses. Neither Democrat Hughes, who served from 1961–69, nor Republican Cahill, who was in office from 1969–73, was ever accused of personal wrongdoing. In fact, Hughes later served a widely praised tenure as chief justice of the New Jersey supreme court.

11. Peirce and Barone, *The Mid-Atlantic States of America*, p. 223.

12. "New Jersey Public Financing: 1985 Gubernatorial Elections," New Jersey Election Law Enforcement Commission, Trenton, September 1986, p. 5.

13. Ibid., p. 10.

14. Ibid., p. 11.

15. Herbert E. Alexander, "Public Financing of State Elections," paper presented at the State of the States Symposium, Eagleton Institute of Politics, Rutgers University, New Brunswick, N.J., December 1989, p. 9.

16. "New Jersey Public Financing: 1985 Gubernatorial Elections," Table D, p. 36. More than 60 percent of the money raised by Shapiro and in excess of 72 percent of the money raised by Kean was from large contributors.

17. Ibid., p. 6.

18. Alexander, "Public Financing of State Elections," p. 14.

19. Herbert E. Alexander and Monica Bauer, *Financing the 1988 Election* (Boulder, Colo.: Westview Press, 1991), Table 3.4, p. 41.

20. Bob Fitzpatrick, "Soft Money on a Hard Roll," *New Jersey Reporter*, Princeton, February 1990, pp. 14–15.

21. Jane Perlez, "TV and Jersey Voting: Ads by State Political Parties Provide New Force in Campaign for Governor," *The New York Times*, October 9, 1981.

22. Fitzpatrick, "Soft Money on a Hard Roll," pp. 17–18.

23. Ibid., p. 14.

24. Ruth S. Jones, "A Decade of U.S. State-level Campaign Finance Reform," paper presented at the Roundtable on Political Finance and Political Corruption of the International Political Science Association, sponsored by the Institute for Political Studies in Japan, Tokyo, September 1989, p. 12.

25. "New Jersey Public Financing: 1991 Gubernatorial Elections," New Jersey Election Law Enforcement Commission, Trenton, p. 24.

26. Joseph F. Sullivan, "Rifle Association under Inquiry over Mailings Endorsing Florio," *The New York Times*, May 23, 1981.

27. "New Jersey Public Financing: 1985 Gubernatorial Elections," pp. 20–21.

28. Alexander, "Public Financing of State Elections," p. 17.

29. A decade after the Bateman–Byrne race, the New Jersey Election Law Enforcement Commission issued a study entitled "Gubernatorial Cost Analysis Report," which noted that New York City television stations were charging as much as $24,000 for a thirty-second political spot in prime time in the fall of 1987, with costs for a similar ad in the Philadelphia market running to $14,000.

30. "New Jersey Public Financing: 1981 Gubernatorial Elections," New Jersey Election Law Enforcement Commission, Trenton, p. 23.

31. Joseph F. Sullivan, "Vote Board Orders Bateman to Pay $100,000 More for Republican Ads," *The New York Times*, October 27, 1981.

32. It should be noted that the Byrne campaign sought to turn this "two-thirds" ruling to its own advantage in the closing days of the race. On November 1, 1977, the Byrne organization filed an amendment to its preelection disclosure report saying that two-thirds of what it characterized as an anti-Bateman radio campaign would be paid for by the Byrne committee, with the remaining third to be picked up by the Democratic State Committee. ELEC disallowed the change, and the Byrne campaign committee went to court. The ELEC ruling was upheld by the New Jersey supreme court just three days before the election.

33. "New Jersey Public Financing: 1985 Gubernatorial Elections," pp. 10–11.

34. Ibid., p. 12.

35. "Trends in Legislative Campaign Financing," p. 4.

36. Jeffrey Kanige, "Money and Power: A Dangerous Brew," *New Jersey Reporter*, Princeton, February 1988, p. 8.

37. "Trends in Legislative Campaign Financing," p. 4.

38. Ibid., pp. 11–12.

39. Ibid., pp. 22–23.

40. Ibid., pp. 43–44.

41. Quoted in Kanige, "Money and Power," p. 9.

42. "Governor's Annual Message," State of New Jersey, Trenton, January 10, 1989, p. 159.

43. "ELEC White Paper: Legislative Public Financing," New Jersey Election Law Enforcement Commission, Trenton, July 1989, pp. 25–26.

44. "Findings and Recommendations of the Ad Hoc Commission on Legislative Ethics and Campaign Finance: A Report to the President of the Senate, the Speaker of the General Assembly and Members of the New Jersey Legislature," Trenton, October 22, 1990, pp. 21–22.

45. Ibid., p. 22.

46. Ibid., p. 13.

47. The state-by-state information in this section is derived from data collected by the Citizens' Research Foundation, Los Angeles, as well as from *Campaign Finance Law 90* (Washington, D.C.: National Clearinghouse on Election Administration, Federal Election Commission, 1990); "State Campaign Finance Laws: The 1990 Legislative Session," *Campaign Practices Reports* 17, no. 15 (July 23, 1990); and Frederick M. Herrmann, *1990 Campaign Finance Update: Legislation and Litigation* (Los Angeles: Citizens' Research Foundation, 1990). Frederick M. Herrmann is executive director of the New Jersey Election Law Enforcement Commission.

48. Jones, "A Decade of U.S. State-level Campaign Finance Reform," p. 19.

49. James Barron, "States Find Income-Tax Checkoffs Aren't Such Easy Money Anymore," *The New York Times*, April 15, 1990; and "State Income Tax Checkoffs," legislative finance paper no. 7, National Conference of State Legislatures, Denver, April 1987, pp. 4–8.

50. Alexander, "Public Financing of State Elections," p. 21.

51. Ibid., p. 19.

52. Ibid., p. 34.

53. Except where otherwise noted, the information in this section is drawn from the Minnesota and Wisconsin sections of Alexander, "Public Financing of State Elections."

54. Telephone interview with Mary Ann McCoy, executive director, Minnesota Ethical Practices Board, October 10, 1990.

55. Alexander, "Public Financing of State Elections," pp. 53–54.

56. "Findings and Recommendations of the Ad Hoc Commission on Legislative Ethics and Campaign Finance," p. 22.

57. Herbert E. Alexander and Michael C. Walker, *Public Financing of Local Elections: A Data Book on Public Funding in Four Cities and Two Counties* (Los Angeles: Citizens' Research Foundation, 1990), p. 4.

58. Ibid.

59. *County of Sacramento v. Fair Political Practices Commission*, 222 Cal. App.3d 687 (1990).

60. *Johnson et al. v. Bradley et al.*, Cal. App.3d (1991); also Frederick M. Muir, "Appeals Court Upholds Campaign Financing Law," *Los Angeles Times*, April 11, 1991.

61. "Dollars and Disclosure: Campaign Finance Reform in New York City (Executive Summary)," New York City Campaign Finance Board, September 1990, p. ix.

62. Koch, Dinkins, Harrison Goldin, and Richard Ravitch, all Democrats, and Republican Rudolph Giuliani participated. Dinkins, after defeating Koch in the Democratic primary, beat Giuliani in the general election. Ronald Lauder, heir to a cosmetics fortune, did not participate and spent a reported $13.7 million—almost four times the program's expenditure ceiling—in an unsuccessful effort to defeat Giuliani in the primary; he then ran as a Conservative party candidate in the general election.

63. "Dollars and Disclosure," Table 4, p. 17.

64. "Trends in Legislative Campaign Financing," p. 2.

65. George Skelton, "Legislators on the Take, Most in Survey Believe," *Los Angeles Times*, January 3, 1990.

# Chapter 3

1. Interview with Keith White, former Columbus bureau chief, Gannett News Service, November 26, 1990.

2. Sandra J. Singer, "The Power of the Purse—It Costs to Run for Legislative Office!!" paper presented at the Western Political Science Association annual meeting, Salt Lake City, March 30–April 1, 1989, p. 2.

3. Ibid.

4. Ruth S. Jones, "A Decade of U.S. State-level Campaign Finance Reform," paper presented at the Roundtable on Political Finance and Political Corruption of the International Political Science Association, sponsored by the Institute for Political Studies in Japan, Tokyo, September 1989, p. 8.

5. "The Paper Chase: A Common Cause/Ohio Study of Improving Access to Campaign Finance Information in the States," Common Cause, Columbus, September 1990, Charts I and IV.

6. See, for example, "1988 California State General Election: Campaign Receipts and Expenditures," Fair Political Practices Commission, Sacramento, 1989.

7. "Summary Report: Campaign Finance Data for 1988 New York State Legislative Elections," New York State Board of Elections, Albany, 1990.

8. Bob Paynter, Keith McKnight, and Andrew Zajac, "State Campaign Fund Masked in Pipeline," *Akron Beacon Journal*, October 1, 1989.

9. Ibid.

10. According to a September 1990 report, South Carolina and Wyoming are the only two states that do not require preelection disclosure. In addition, thirty-six states require disclosure reports at least twice between the primary and the general election. "Campaign Finance Reform in the States," Common Cause, Washington, D.C., September 1990.

11. Ruth S. Jones, "Financing State Elections," in *Money and Politics in the United States: Financing Elections in the 1980s*, ed. Michael J. Malbin (Chatham, N.J.: Chatham House Publishers, 1984), pp. 209–10.

12. Keith McKnight and Andrew Zajac, "Dipping into Campaign Kitty,"*Akron Beacon Journal*, September 23, 1990.

13. This ruling came as part of the Supreme Court's decision in *Buckley v. Valeo*, 424 U.S. 1 (1976).

14. Robert J. Huckshorn, "Who Gave It? Who Got It? The Enforcement of Campaign Finance Laws in the States," *Journal of Politics* 47, no. 3 (August 1985): 787.

15. Jones, "A Decade of U.S. State-level Campaign Finance Reform," p. 9.

16. "Eu, Supporters Fined $20,000 for Reports Filed 2 Years Late," *Los Angeles Times*, December 5, 1990.

17. Letter to Herbert E. Alexander from Gregory E. Nagy, legal director, New Jersey Election Law Enforcement Commission, November 16, 1990.

18. Jones, "A Decade of U.S. State-level Campaign Finance Reform," p. 24.

19. Frank J. Sorauf, *Money in American Elections* (Glenview, Ill.: Scott, Foresman and Co., 1988), p. 290.

20. "Political committee" here includes political action committees but also political party committees and possibly some issue committees.

21. See, for example, a study of trends in campaign spending related to general and mass media advertising inflation: "Gubernatorial Cost Analysis Report," New Jersey Election Law Enforcement Commission, Trenton, June 1988.

22. "Trends in Legislative Campaign Financing: 1977–1987," white paper no. 2, New Jersey Election Law Enforcement Commission, Trenton, May 1989.

23. "Legislative Public Financing," white paper no. 3, New Jersey Election Law Enforcement Commission, Trenton, July 1989.

24. "1989 Overview of Groups, Political Parties and PACs," Alaska Public Officers Commission, Anchorage, March 1990.

25. "Political Spending by Major Interest Groups in Washington State, 1988–1989," Public Disclosure Commission, Olympia, January 1990.

26. By virtue of a constitutional requirement of $1 million annually, adjusted for cost-of-living changes. Political Reform Act of 1974, California Government Code sec. 83122.

27. "1989 Annual Report," New Jersey Election Law Enforcement Commission, Trenton, 1990, p. 12.

28. Ibid., p. 6.

29. Letter to author from Gregory E. Nagy, November 16, 1990.

30. "1989 Annual Report," New Jersey Election Law Enforcement Commission, pp. 12–13.

31. Ibid., p. 11.

32. "Findings and Recommendations of the Ad Hoc Commission on Legislative Ethics and Campaign Finance: A Report to the President of the Senate, the Speaker of the General Assembly and Members of the New Jersey Legislature," Trenton, October 22, 1990, p. 18.

33. In Wisconsin's system of public financing, conduit contributions are used to get around the disincentives against the acceptance of PAC money.

34. "Clean Up the Laundry," editorial, *Cleveland Plain Dealer*, October 3, 1989.

35. Paynter, McKnight, and Zajac, "State Campaign Funds Masked in Pipeline."

36. "Campaign Finance Reform in the States," Common Cause, Washington, D.C., September 1990, p. 59.

37. Jones, "A Decade of U.S. State-level Campaign Finance Reform," p. 15.

38. Chris Haughee, "The Florida Election Campaign Financing Act: A Bold Approach to Public Financing of Elections," *Florida State University Law*

*Review* 14, no. 3 (Fall 1986): 585–605; also see Herbert E. Alexander and Mike Eberts, *Public Financing of State Elections: A Data Book on Tax-assisted Funding of Political Parties and Candidates in Twenty States* (Los Angeles: Citizens' Research Foundation, 1986), pp. 27–28.

39. Data received from Eric D. Prutsman, Division of Elections, Florida Department of State, October 20, 1989.

40. Alexander and Eberts, *Public Financing of State Elections*, pp. 227–39.

41. Opinion no. 81-004, Maryland attorney general, February 9, 1981.

42. Interview with Phil Andrews, executive director of Common Cause of Maryland, November 27, 1990.

43. "Maryland: Governor Looks to Sweep Out Public Campaign Fund," *COGEL Guardian* 10, no. 2, Council on Governmental Ethics Laws, Lexington, Ky., April 30, 1989, p. 12.

44. Interview with Phil Andrews, November 27, 1990.

45. Interview with Phil West, executive director, Common Cause of Rhode Island, March 1, 1991.

46. Ibid.

47. Scott MacKay, "Would-Be Governors Spent over $10 Million on Election," *Providence Journal-Bulletin,* December 9, 1990.

48. Interview with Phil West.

49. This narrative follows Herbert E. Alexander, "California's Mixed Signals on Election Reform," prepared for the Public Affairs Council, Washington, D.C., July 1988, pp. 1–15.

50. Jake Henshaw and Jeanine Guttman, "Good Triumphs over BAD in California," *Campaigns & Elections,* August/September 1988, pp. 11–12.

51. Quoted in Alexander, "California's Mixed Signals on Election Reform," p. 1.

52. Richard C. Paddock, "Judge Strikes Down Prop. 73 Funding Limits," *Los Angeles Times,* September 26, 1990; *Service Employees International Union v. Fair Political Practices Commission,* U.S. District Court, Eastern District of California, no. CIV. S-89-433 LKK.

53. Quoted in Paul Jacobs, "Ruling Has Political Consultants Reeling," *Los Angeles Times,* September 27, 1990.

54. Richard C. Paddock, "Contribution Limits for Legislative Races Restored," Los Angeles Times, September 29, 1990.

55. Dan Morain, "Ruling Helps Feinstein Raise $750,000," *Los Angeles Times,* October 4, 1990.

56. Quoted in Richard C. Paddock, "Boost to Political Underdogs Seen," *Los Angeles Times,* September 27, 1990.

57. Philip Hager and Richard C. Paddock, "Proposition with Most Votes Would Nullify Rival One," *Los Angeles Times,* November 2, 1990; *Taxpayers to Limit Campaign Spending v. Fair Political Practices Commission,* State of California Supreme Court S012016, November 1, 1990.

58. Quoted in Hager and Paddock, "Proposition with Most Votes Would Nullify Rival One."

59. "Propositions 68 and 73," *FPPC Bulletin*, Fair Political Practices Commission, Sacramento, December 1990, pp. 6–7.

60. *County of Sacramento v. Fair Political Practices Commission*, 222 Cal. App.3d 687 (1990).

61. *State of Florida v. Jack P. Dodd*, no. 75,788, May 8, 1990, p. 11.

62. Ibid., p. 8.

63. "Campaign Finance Reform in the States," pp. 47–48.

64. Ibid., p. 48.

65. "The Gang that Shot John Durkin," *PACs & Lobbies*, November 21, 1990, pp. 1, 4.

66. Glen Craney, "Minnesota Steals the Spotlight on Campaign-Finance Reform," *Congressional Quarterly* 48, no. 17 (April 28, 1990): 1240–41.

67. Robert B. Hawkins, Jr., "Pre-emption: The Dramatic Rise of Federal Supremacy," *Journal of State Government* 63, no. 1 (January–March 1990): 10–13.

# Chapter 4

1. Quoted in "COGEL Drafts Model State Law for Campaign Finance, Ethics and Lobbying," *Campaign Practices Reports* 17, no. 21 (October 15, 1990): 5; "A Model Law for Campaign Finance, Ethics and Lobbying Regulation," proposed draft for adoption, Council on Governmental Ethics Laws, Lexington, Ky., July 1990, 22 pp.

2. *Buckley v. Valeo*, 424 U.S. 1 (1976).

3. Ruth S. Jones, "A Decade of U.S. State-level Campaign Finance Reform," paper presented at the Roundtable on Political Finance and Political Corruption of the International Political Science Association, sponsored by the Institute for Political Studies in Japan, Tokyo, September 1989, p. 1.

4. For a proposal concerning a "Uniform Campaign Disclosure Code" to cover soft money disclosure, see "Soft Money—A Loophole for the '80s," Center for Responsive Politics, Washington, D.C., 1985, p. 24.

5. Telephone interview with Dale Perry, political correspondent, *Greenville Piedmont* (South Carolina), December 3, 1990.

6. Cited in Frederick M. Herrmann, *1990 Campaign Finance Update: Legislation and Litigation* (Los Angeles: Citizens' Research Foundation, 1990), p. 50. The report published by the North Carolina Center for Public Policy Research is entitled "Campaign Disclosure Laws: An Analysis of Campaign Finance Disclosure in North Carolina and an Analysis of 50 State Campaign Reporting Laws."

7. David S. Broder, "Assessing Campaign Reform: Lessons for the Future," in *Campaign Money: Reform and Reality in the States*, ed. Herbert E. Alexander (New York: Macmillan Publishing Co., 1976), p. 313.

8. Bill Boyarsky, "New Panels for Local Campaign Reforms Urged," *Los Angeles Times*, August 27, 1989.

9. Ibid.

10. "Legislatures in the States: Progress, Problems and Possibilities," report of the Symposium on the Legislature in the Twenty-first Century, Williamsburg, Va., April 1990, sponsored by the Eagleton Institute of Politics, Rutgers University, New Brunswick, N.J., p. 7.

11. "Independent Expenditures: A Growing Phenomenon in California Political Campaigns," report of Secretary of State March Fong Eu, Sacramento, July 1991, pp. i–ii.

12. The primary case here is *First National Bank of Boston v. Bellotti*, 435 U.S. 765 (1978), in which the Supreme Court ruled unconstitutional a Massachusetts law prohibiting corporations from spending money on ballot issues that did not pertain directly to their corporate interests.

13. Kenneth Reich, "The 64-Million Dollar Question," *Campaigns & Elections*, March/April 1989, p. 15.

14. Don M. Millis, "The Best Laid Schemes of Mice and Men: Campaign Finance Reform Gone Awry," *Wisconsin Law Review* 1989, no. 6 (1989): 1474.

15. U.S. Supreme Court Lets Stand Wisconsin Cap on PAC Donations," *Campaign Practices Reports* 17, no. 24 (December 10, 1990): 5.

16. Millis, "The Best Laid Schemes of Mice and Men," pp. 1484–85. Conduit contributions are unique to Wisconsin. In lieu of corporate or labor contributions, conduit contributions are a form of payroll deduction in which employees can specify contributions to be set aside without designating a recipient candidate until a later date. Unlike PAC contributions, conduit contributions are considered to be bundled individual contributions and count toward the candidate's eligibility threshold; hence special interest money is being funneled increasingly through this mechanism to candidates throughout the state. Like PACs, conduits must disclose their receipts and disbursements.

17. Ibid., p. 1487.

18. "The Price of Political Power: Arizona State Legislative Races, 1988," United for Arizona, Phoenix, n.d., p. 3.

19. Report of the Office of Campaign and Political Finance of the Commonwealth of Massachusetts, Boston, January 29, 1987, p. 10.

20. Quoted in "COGEL Drafts Model State Law for Campaign Finance, Ethics & Lobbying," p. 5.

21. Broder, "Assessing Campaign Reform," pp. 314–15.

22. Herbert E. Alexander, "Public Financing of State Elections," paper presented at the State of the States Symposium, Eagleton Institute of Politics, Rutgers University, New Brunswick, N.J., December 1989, p. 50.

23. "Declining Public Participation in Tax Checkoff Threatens Presidential Fund," *Campaign Practices Reports* 16, no. 18 (September 18, 1989): 5.

24. Alexander, "Public Financing of State Elections," p. 52.

25. Broder, "Assessing Campaign Reform," p. 316.

26. Alexander, "Public Financing of State Elections," p. 43.

27. Data provided by Raymond E. Wallace, executive director, Kentucky Registry of Election Finance, October 26, 1990; additional data provided by Professor Joel Goldstein, University of Louisville, November 30, 1990.

28. "Findings and Recommendations of the Ad Hoc Commission on Legislative Ethics and Campaign Finance: A Report to the President of the Senate, the Speaker of the General Assembly and Members of the New Jersey Legislature," Trenton, October 22, 1990, p. 13.

29. Larry J. Sabato, *The Party's Just Begun* (Glenview, Ill.: Scott, Foresman/Little, Brown, 1988), p. 21.

30. "Legislatures in the States," p. 7.

## Appendix 1
### Public Financing and Tax-Assisted Funding in State Elections

| | System | | Benefits | | | Elections | | Year |
|---|---|---|---|---|---|---|---|---|
| | Checkoff | Add-on | Governor | Other Offices | Parties | General | Primary | Year Enacted |
| AL | | ✓ | | | | | | 1983 |
| AZ | | ✓ | | | ✓ | | | 1988 |
| CA | | ✓ | | | ✓ | | | 1982 |
| FL | legislative appropriation | | ✓ | ✓ | | ✓ | ✓ | 1986 |
| HI | ✓ | | ✓ | ✓ | | ✓ | ✓ | 1978-79 |
| ID | ✓ | | | | ✓ | | | 1975 |
| IN | license plate revenues | | | | ✓ | | | 1977 |
| IA | ✓ | | | | ✓ | | | 1973 |
| KY | ✓ | | | | ✓ | | | 1976 |
| ME | | ✓ | ✓ | | ✓ | | | 1973 |
| MD | | ✓ | ✓ | ✓ | | ✓ | ✓ | 1974 |
| MA | | ✓ | ✓ | | | ✓ | ✓ | 1975 |
| MI | ✓ | | ✓ | | | ✓ | ✓ | 1976 |
| MN | ✓ | | ✓ | | | ✓ | | 1974 |
| MT | | ✓ | ✓ | ✓ | | ✓ | | 1975 |
| NH | filing fee waiver | | ✓ | ✓ | | ✓ | | 1987 |
| NJ | ✓ | | ✓ | ✓ | | ✓ | ✓ | 1974 |
| NC | ✓ | | ✓ | | ✓ | ✓ | | 1975/1988 |
| OH | ✓ | | | | ✓ | | | 1987 |
| RI | checkoff & legislative appropriation | | ✓ | | ✓ | ✓ | | 1973/1988 |
| UT | ✓ | | ✓ | | ✓ | | | 1973 |
| VA | | ✓ | ✓ | ✓ | | ✓ | | 1982 |
| WI | ✓ | | ✓ | | | ✓ | | 1977 |

Source: Citizens' Research Foundation.

Notes: Oklahoma enacted legislation, but its program has been discontinued. Some party funding may go to candidates in specific election campaigns, but in most states, parties are prohibited from engaging in primary election activity. In 1982, Maryland suspended its add-on, but it will disburse previously collected funds in the 1994 gubernatorial election. In 1987, the Oregon legislature enacted an income-tax-based political party add-on, long after a tax checkoff ended in 1981 due to a "sunset" provision. In 1989, New Hampshire enacted a filing fee waiver for state and federal candidates. In 1988, North Carolina enacted a "candidates financing fund" with an add-on system that operates separately from the "political parties fund" checkoff established in 1975. In 1988, Rhode Island enacted a gubernatorial election fund to be financed by general appropriations in lieu of sufficient checkoff participation.

**Appendix 2A**
**State Political Finance Regulation, 1990:**
**State Disclosure Laws**

| | Disclosure Requirements | Contribution Limits (Individuals) | Contribution Limits (Organizations) | Tax Credit/ Deduction | Independent Election Agency |
|---|---|---|---|---|---|
| AL | Yes | No | Yes | No | No |
| AK | Yes | Yes | Yes | No | Yes |
| AZ | Yes | Yes | Yes | Yes[a] | No |
| AR | Yes | Yes | Yes | No | Yes[e] |
| CA | Yes | Yes[c] | Yes[c] | Yes[b] | Yes |
| CO | Yes | No | No | No | No |
| CT | Yes | Yes | Yes | No | Yes |
| DE | Yes | Yes | Yes | No | Yes |
| FL | Yes | Yes | Yes | No | Yes |
| GA | Yes | Yes | Yes | No | Yes |
| HI | Yes | Yes | Yes | Yes[a] | Yes |
| ID | Yes | No | No | No | No |
| IL | Yes | No[d] | No | No | Yes |
| IN | Yes | No | Yes | No | Yes |
| IA | Yes | No | Yes | No | Yes |
| KS | Yes | Yes | Yes | No | Yes |
| KY | Yes | Yes | Yes | No | Yes |
| LA | Yes | Yes | Yes | No | Yes |
| ME | Yes | Yes | Yes | No | Yes |
| MD | Yes | Yes | Yes | No | Yes |
| MA | Yes | Yes | Yes | No | Yes |
| MI | Yes | Yes | Yes | No | No |
| MN | Yes | Yes | Yes | Yes[b] | Yes |
| MS | Yes | No | Yes | No | No |
| MO | Yes | No | No | No | No |
| MT | Yes | Yes | Yes | Yes[a] | Yes |
| NE | Yes | No | No | No | Yes |
| NV | Yes | No | No | No | No |
| NH | Yes | Yes | Yes | No | No |
| NJ | Yes | Yes[f] | Yes[f] | No | Yes |
| NM | Yes | No | No | No | No |
| NY | Yes | Yes | Yes | No | Yes |
| NC | Yes | Yes | Yes | Yes[a] | Yes |
| ND | Yes | No | Yes | No | No |
| OH | Yes | No | Yes | No | No |
| OK | Yes | Yes | Yes | Yes[a] | Yes |
| OR | Yes | No | No | Yes[b] | No |
| PA | Yes | No | Yes | No | No |
| RI | Yes | Yes | Yes | No | Yes |
| SC | Yes[g] | No | No | No | Yes |
| SD | Yes | Yes | Yes | No | No |
| TN | Yes | No | Yes | No | Yes |
| TX | Yes | No | Yes | No | No |
| UT | Yes | No | No | No | No |
| VT | Yes | Yes | Yes | No | No |
| VA | Yes | No | No | No | Yes |
| WA | Yes | Yes | Yes | No | Yes |
| WV | Yes | Yes | Yes | No | No |
| WI | Yes | Yes | Yes | No | Yes |
| WY | Yes[g] | Yes | Yes | No | No |

**Appendix 2A** (Cont'd)

Sources: *Campaign Finance Law 90* (Washington, D.C.: National Clearinghouse on Election Administration, Federal Election Commission, 1990); "State Campaign Finance Laws: The 1990 Legislative Session," *Campaign Practices Reports* vol.17, no. 15 (July 23, 1990); Frederick M. Herrmann, *1990 Campaign Finance Update: Legislation and Litigation* (Los Angeles: Citizens' Research Foundation, 1990); Ronald D. Michaelson, *1989 Campaign Finance Update: Legislation and Litigation* (Los Angeles: Citizens' Research Foundation, 1990); Ronald D. Michaelson, *1988 Campaign Finance Update: Legislation and Litigation,* prepared for the Council on Governmental Ethics Laws (COGEL), Lexington, Ky., 1988.

a. Tax deduction.

b. Tax credit.

c. For legislative campaigns only, but under litigation.

d. The one restriction in Illinois prohibits any individual who owns 5 percent or more of the stock in a horse racing organization from making political donations.

e. A campaign finance initiative passed by Arkansas voters in November 1990 creates a five-member Arkansas Ethics Commission effective January 1, 1991, to administer both the new campaign finance statute and a public ethics law passed by voters in 1988.

f. New Jersey's individual and organizational contribution limits apply only to the state's publicly funded gubernatorial election. There are currently no contribution limits in state legislative races.

g. Unlike the other forty-eight states, which require both pre- and postelection reporting, South Carolina and Wyoming mandate only postelection filing. South Carolina does require that, two weeks prior to the election, candidates make a list of those contributing $100 or more available upon request. However, one must request such a list of the candidate's headquarters; it is not filed with the state.

## Appendix 2B
## Political Finance Regulation, 1990:
## State Limits on Selected Contributions

| | Corporate Contributions | | | Union Contributions | | | PAC Contributions | | |
|---|---|---|---|---|---|---|---|---|---|
| | Prohibit | Limit | Unlimited | Prohibit | Limit | Unlimited | Prohibit | Limit | Unlimited |
| AL | | ✓ | | | | ✓ | | | ✓ |
| AK | | ✓ | | | ✓ | | ✓ | | |
| AZ | ✓ | | | ✓ | | | | ✓ | |
| AR | | ✓ | | | ✓ | | ✓ | | |
| CA | | | ✓a | | | ✓ | | | ✓ |
| CO | | ✓ | | | ✓ | | | | ✓ |
| CT | ✓ | | | ✓ | | | | ✓ | |
| DE | | ✓ | | | ✓ | | | ✓ | |
| FL | | ✓ | | | ✓ | | | ✓ | |
| GA | | ✓ | | | ✓ | | | ✓ | |
| HI | | ✓ | | | ✓ | | | ✓ | |
| ID | | | ✓ | | | ✓ | | | ✓ |
| IL | | | ✓ | | | ✓ | | | ✓ |
| IN | | ✓ | | | ✓ | | | | ✓ |
| IA | ✓ | | | | | ✓ | | | ✓ |
| KS | | ✓ | | | ✓ | | | ✓ | |
| KY | ✓ | | | | | ✓ | | ✓ | |
| LA | | ✓ | | | ✓ | | | ✓ | |
| ME | | ✓ | | | ✓ | | | ✓ | |
| MD | | ✓ | | | ✓ | | | | ✓ |
| MA | ✓ | | | | | ✓ | | ✓ | |
| MI | ✓ | | | | ✓ | | | ✓ | |
| MN | ✓ | | | | ✓ | | | ✓ | |
| MS | | ✓ | | | | ✓ | | | ✓ |
| MO | | | ✓ | | | ✓ | | | ✓ |
| MT | ✓ | | | | ✓ | | | ✓ | |
| NE | | | ✓ | | | ✓ | | | ✓ |
| NV | | | ✓ | | | ✓ | | | ✓ |
| NH | ✓ | | | ✓ | | | | ✓ | |
| NJ | | ✓b | | | ✓b | | | ✓ | |
| NM | | | ✓ | | | ✓ | | | ✓ |
| NY | | ✓ | | | | ✓ | | | ✓ |
| NC | ✓ | | | ✓ | | | | ✓ | |
| ND | ✓ | | | ✓ | | | | | ✓ |
| OH | ✓ | | | | | ✓ | | | ✓ |
| OK | ✓ | | | | ✓ | | | ✓ | |
| OR | | | ✓ | | | ✓ | | | ✓ |
| PA | ✓ | | | ✓ | | | | | ✓ |
| RI | | ✓ | | | ✓ | | | ✓ | |
| SC | | | ✓ | | | ✓ | | | ✓ |
| SD | ✓ | | | | ✓ | | | | ✓ |
| TN | ✓ | | | | | ✓ | | | ✓ |
| TX | ✓ | | | ✓ | | | | | ✓ |
| UT | | | ✓ | | | ✓ | | | ✓ |
| VT | | ✓ | | | | ✓ | | ✓ | |
| VA | | | ✓ | | | ✓ | | | ✓ |
| WA | | ✓ | | | ✓ | | | ✓ | |
| WV | ✓ | | | | ✓ | | | ✓ | |
| WI | ✓ | | | ✓ | | | | ✓ | |
| WY | ✓ | | | ✓ | | | | | ✓ |

**Appendix 2B** (Cont'd)

Sources: *Campaign Finance Law 90* (Washington, D.C.: National Clearinghouse on Election Administration, Federal Election Commission, 1990); "State Campaign Finance Laws: The 1990 Legislative Session," *Campaign Practices Reports* vol. 17, no. 15 (July 23, 1990); Frederick M. Herrmann, *1990 Campaign Finance Update: Legislation and Litigation* (Los Angeles: Citizens' Research Foundation, 1990); Ronald D. Michaelson, *1989 Campaign Finance Update: Legislation and Litigation* (Los Angeles: Citizens' Research Foundation, 1990); Ronald D. Michaelson, *1988 Campaign Finance Update: Legislation and Litigation,* prepared for the Council on Governmental Ethics Laws (COGEL), Lexington, Ky., 1988.

[a] Limits apply to legislative campaigns only, but under litigation.

[b] Limits apply to gubernatorial campaigns only.

## Appendix 3
## Election Reform and Public Financing Ballot Measures

| State/Locality | Date | Ballot Issue | Outcome |
|---|---|---|---|
| Washington | November 1972 | Initiative 276 | Passed<br>822,360 for (68%)<br>370,461 against<br>(provided campaign finance and lobbyist disclosure) |
| California | June 1974 | Proposition 9 | Passed<br>3,224,765 for (69%)<br>1,392,783 against<br>(constitutional amendment entitled the Political Reform Act of 1974; established the Fair Political Practices Commission and covered disclosure of political funds, lobbying and personal finance disclosure by candidates and public officials) |
| Oregon | May 1976 | Measure no. 7 | Failed<br>263,738 for (29%)<br>659,327 against<br>(would have reimbursed qualified candidates for certain eligible campaign expenditures, within set limits during general elections only) |
| Florida | November 1976 | Sunshine Amendment | Passed<br>1,765,626 for (79%)<br>461,940 against<br>(constitutional amendment gave the Commission on Ethics independent status and combined responsibility for ethics and financial disclosure) |
| Hawaii | November 1978 | Two issues from constitutional convention | Passed both:<br>campaign financing including partial public funding<br>145,907 for (57%)<br>106,316 against<br>candidates' personal finances<br>179,958 for (71%)<br>72,265 against |

| State/Locality | Date | Ballot Issue | Outcome |
|---|---|---|---|
| Minnesota | November 1980 | Constitutional amendment | Passed<br>1,457,454 for (78%)<br>398,551 against<br>(approved amendments already enacted by the state legislature, providing for disclosure, some contribution and expenditure limitations, and increases in the tax checkoff and the amount of public funding) |
| California | November 1984 | Proposition 40 | Failed<br>3,109,746 for (35%)<br>5,640,473 against<br>(would have banned corporate and labor union contributions to candidates and imposed a $1,000 annual limit on campaign gifts from PACs and others) |
| Los Angeles | April 1985 | Charter Amendment I | Passed<br>303,950 for (76%)<br>91,551 against<br>(imposed contribution limits on citywide and city council campaigns) |
| Tucson | November 1985 | Proposition 105 | Passed<br>30,996 for (52%)<br>28,243 against<br>(provided public funding in campaigns for mayor and city council) |
| Arizona | November 1986 | Proposition 200 | Passed<br>526,640 for (64%)<br>284,122 against<br>(imposed contribution limits and aggregate limits on PAC contributions) |
| Rhode Island | November 1986 | Question 6 | Passed<br>143,973 for (53%)<br>125,964 against<br>(directed state legislature to enact laws within eighteen months pertaining to a constitutional convention and containing both public financing and ethics provisions) |
| Sacramento County, California[a] | November 1986 | Measure A | Passed<br>153,133 for (61%)<br>97,131 against<br>(provided public funding in campaigns for county elective office) |

| State/Locality | Date | Ballot Issue | Outcome |
|---|---|---|---|
| California | June 1988 | Proposition 68 | Passed<br>2,802,614 for (53%)<br>2,501,263 against<br>(sought to reform state legislative campaigns by a system of public funding and expenditure limits) |
| | | Proposition 73 | Passed<br>3,144,944 for (58%)<br>2,271,941 against<br>(prohibited public funding and provided firm contribution limits at all levels) |
| New York City | November 1988 | Proposal 2 | Passed<br>846,085 for (86%)<br>132,589 against<br>(established standards for government ethics and conflicts of interest; prohibited certain types of conduct) |
| | | Proposal 6 | Passed<br>763,474 for (79%)<br>198,549 against<br>(reinforced law earlier enacted by city council; established public financing program including expenditure limits; established Campaign Finance Board) |
| King County, Washington | November 1989 | Charter Amendment I | Passed<br>179,941 for (52%)<br>166,087 against<br>(required the County Council to establish by ordinance a system for distributing public matching funds to qualified candidates for county elective offices, mandatory campaign contribution limits, and penalties for the violations of the mandatory contribution limits or voluntary expenditure limits) |
| Maine | November 1989 | "An Act to Limit Spending and Contributions in Campaigns for Governor" | Failed<br>98,148 for (44%)<br>125,562 against<br>(would have authorized spending and contribution limits and would have created public matching fund system similar to the presidential system) |

| State/Locality[a] | Date | Ballot Issue | Outcome |
|---|---|---|---|
| Los Angeles[a] | June 1990 | Charter Amendment H | Passed<br>204,746 for (57%)<br>159,519 against<br>(provided public matching funds for certain city candidates. Public funds tied to expenditure limits are given only to qualified candidates in competitive races. Tightened restrictions on all political committees, and barred candidates from making decisions on issues involving campaign contributors for a year after receiving contributions) |
| Arkansas | November 1990 | "Standards of Conduct and Disclosure Act for Candidates and Political Campaigns" | Passed<br>355,957 for (65%)<br>186,204 against<br>(tightened contribution limits, expanded disclosure, restricted times when candidates can raise funds, and created an independent commission to enforce the law) |
| California | November 1990 | Proposition 131 | Failed<br>2,718,292 for (38%)<br>4,477,356 against<br>(would have combined term limitations with a system of public funding, expenditure ceilings, and contribution limits) |
| Massachusetts | November 1990 | Proposition 6 | Passed<br>1,141,706 for (54%)<br>973,933 against<br>(asked whether broadcast outlets in the state should be compelled to give free and equal time to candidates for public office. This was a nonbinding vote with no legal impact, given federal jurisdiction over such matters) |
| Sacramento[a] | November 1990 | Measure W offered by City Council | Passed<br>60,222 for (63%)<br>35,812 against<br>(nonbinding vote sought to ascertain whether city residents favored a system of partial public financing combined with contribution and spending limits) |

| Totals: | City Measures: | 5 on ballot, | 5 passed |
|---|---|---|---|
| | Country Measures: | 2 on ballot, | 2 passed |
| | State Measures: | 15 on ballot, | 11 passed |
| | Overall: | 22 on ballot, | 18 passed |

Source: Citizens' Research Foundation.

a  Under litigation

# Index